DOCKLANDS LIGHT RAILWAY

JAMES ABBOTT

MODERN **RAILWAYS** SPECIAL

LONDON

IAN ALLAN LTD

First published 1991

ISBN 0 7110 2024 8

© Ian Allan Ltd 1991

Published by Ian Allan Ltd, Shepperton, Surrey; and printed by Ian Allan Printing Ltd at their works at Coombelands in Runnymede, England.

British Library Cataloguing in Publication Data

Abbott, James
    Docklands light railway. — (Modern Railways special)
    I. Title   II. Series
    385.509421

Previous page:
Poplar Depot, 30 July 1987. *Brian Morrison*

Below:
Island Gardens station: this will be replaced by an underground station when the Lewisham extension opens. *Brian Morrison*

CONTENTS

Front cover:
Shadwell on 31 May 1990 with unit 01 forming a Tower Gateway-Island Gardens service. *John Glover*

Back cover:
Unit 11 was used to carry Her Majesty The Queen on the opening day, 30 July 1987. *DLR*

INTRODUCTION

THIS is the story of the creation of Britain's first automated urban railway. It is a story of transformation: from nothing to an innovative 7.5-mile system in just three years, and from there to a system twice the size that forms an integral part of the transport network of East London. It is a story of transformation in the surroundings of the railway, too: from deserted wharves and warehouses to a glittering hub of the world financial industry — a transformation largely made possible by the presence of the railway. It is not only the moneyed developers who have benefited: in surveys, longstanding residents of the Isle of Dogs cite the light railway as the single most important transformation wrought by the London Docklands Development Corporation.

The sums involved have spiralled. The initial railway was built for a bargain basement £77 million, but now more than 10 times that sum is being spent on the Docklands Light Railway (DLR). A new tunnel has been built to Bank (£250 million), a new line to Beckton (another £250 million), there are new trains, new signalling, new stations — and now a new line to Lewisham.

Adding all these bits on while still trying to run a service on the existing system has been not unlike trying to turn a mini into a double-decker bus — on the move. Inevitably, the ride has been somewhat bumpy during installation of the metaphorical stairs, bells and destination blinds, but when it is all finished there should be a lot more room for passengers to travel in comfort. Capacity will have been increased by more than seven times what was originally planned.

That bumpy ride notwithstanding, the DLR has been a tremendous success: it was built at very little cost to the taxpayer, and at a speed more often associated with the Far East than the East End. It has achieved one of its prime goals, reviving the devastated Docklands area, beyond the wildest dreams that anyone had when it was first conceived. That so much work has been done on the railway since it opened is a symbol of its success, not its failure, as it strives to keep up with the development it has generated.

My thanks to those in the DLR and elsewhere who have given their time to tell me of the twists and turns in the story.

James Abbott
London, January 1991

Below:
The shadow of the huge new office tower at Canary Wharf looms over the DLR delta junction in this January 1991 view. Civil engineering work on upgrading the junction can be seen in the background. *Brian Morrison*

1: THE DLR CONCEPT IS BORN

THE Docklands are an area of London with a rich and colourful history. With a long seafaring tradition stretching back to 16th century expeditions which set out down the River Thames from Wapping in bids to find the northeast and northwest passages to Asia, the area came into its own when the coming of Empire turned London into a hub of world trade.

The West India Docks on the Isle of Dogs opened in 1802, and were London's first purpose-built trading docks and the greatest civil engineering structure of their day. They had a 21-year monopoly on trade with the West Indies, an arrangement that was repeated in the Asian trade for the East India Docks, opened four years later. As the entrepôt trade expanded, docks spread along the river: Thomas Telford's St Katharine Dock at Wapping opened in 1828, and on the Surrey side the Greenland Dock was enlarged. Industry sprang up alongside the wharves, and a spider's web of railway lines was spun over the whole area.

Railway developers were behind the building of the first of the 'Royal' docks, the Victoria Dock, which was specifically designed for steamships and opened in 1855. Nearer the mouth of the Thames than the earlier docks, the Victoria Dock captured much of their trade and was followed by the Albert Dock in 1880. The King George V Dock, opened in 1921, completed the royal docks, which enclosed 245 acres of water and were the greatest docks complex in the world.

After World War 2, the London docks entered a protracted period of decline as

Above right:
Docklands as was: Ben Line vessel *Benvrackie* at West India Dock in 1957, with a PLA locomotive in the foreground. The PLA used 0-4-0 tanks in the West India Docks due to the tight curvature of the sidings there. *Courtesy of Museum in Docklands, PLA Collection*

Right:
The Docks in 1983, prior to revival: Canary and Heron wharves. The warehouses at left have been swept away and replaced by the new Canary Wharf office complex. *John Glover*

trade moved down-river to the new container port at Tilbury. The East India Docks closed in 1967 and the Surrey Docks in 1970, while the West India and Millwall Docks hung on until 1980 and the Royals until 1981. The principal source of employment of the waterfront communities was gone and unemployment climbed, reaching a level of 24% when the 'Royals' closed.

Urgent action was called for, and in 1981 the Government set up the London Docklands Development Corporation (LDDC) with the aim of regenerating the area. At the same time an enterprise zone — a district with valuable tax breaks for employers intended to harness the same dynamic forces of capitalism that led to the building of the docks in the last century — was declared on the Isle of Dogs.

One of the first tasks facing the new development corporation was to renew the outdated infrastructure in Docklands. Transport in particular was a priority area, as difficulties of access from other parts of London and the rest of the country were a serious disincentive to new employers. Public transport provision was poor — as had been recognised for some time by London Transport, the Greater London Council and the local authorities — and the new development corporation added its weight to the effort to get something done about it.

Earlier efforts
Extension of a branch of the Bakerloo Line to the Docks had been a goal of transport planners ever since the 1940s. Realisation came a step closer when a new tube tunnel was bored in the late 1970s from Baker Street to Charing Cross, through which trains off the Bakerloo's Stanmore branch were diverted; the new railway was named the 'Jubilee Line'. There were various plans for extending this line eastwards through

the City and on to Docklands, with a principal aim being to stitch together the two sides of the river in east London, where cross-river links were poor.

To this end, prices were sought in 1977 for a tunnel under the river linking the Royal Docks with Woolwich. The tunnel would have been to British Rail loading gauge, the idea being to extend the BR line to North Woolwich south of the river in advance of the arrival of the Jubilee Line from the City. Just as prices were coming in for the tunnel, it became apparent that strictures on public spending would prevent early eastwards extension of the Jubilee Line, and the cross-river project was dropped. Cancellation of the Jubilee Line extension left Docklands as much out on a limb as ever.

Meanwhile, London Transport had set up a project team that was looking at light rail systems on the Continent, such as the Amsterdam tram system, with a view to possible applications in the British capital. Ideas investigated included an automatic 'peoplemover' from Hatton Cross to the new Terminal 4 at Heathrow Airport (which was discarded in favour of a single-track extension to the Piccadilly Line), and trams between Finsbury Park and Muswell Hill, and Croydon and New Addington (routes for which light rail is still proposed today).

In 1980, the team proposed an automated light rail system for Docklands. A line from Aldgate East to Beckton, with a possible branch from Limehouse to the Isle of Dogs, was suggested. At its western end,

Below:
1980 thoughts on a rapid transit system for Docklands. Beckton was the primary objective, and the line would have looped under Aldgate East Underground station in tunnel. *Courtesy London Transport.*

the line would have had a 1km single-track tube tunnel, serving a platform underneath the District Line platforms at Aldgate East. This scheme progressed to the point where manufacturers were taking a serious interest in it: Metro Cammell of Birmingham linked up with UTDC of Canada to offer a proposal based on linear induction motors, while Hawker Siddeley Rail Projects and GEC put up counter proposals. LT began negotiations with BR about using part of the viaduct out of Fenchurch Street for the new automated railway.

DLR authorised
When the LDDC came on the scene, a further look was taken at the light rail idea. A report entitled *Public Transport Provision for Docklands* was prepared by the LDDC, the GLC, LT and civil servants from the Departments of Environment, Trade & Industry, and Transport, and sent for consideration by the Government in June 1982.

The report looked at an express bus system for Docklands, along with a north-south and east-west railway. For the rail option, a modern Continental-style tram system was envisaged, with overhead catenary and a mixture of segregated and on-street running; the northern end of the railway involved some street running along the Mile End Road to reach a terminus at Mile End Underground station.

In straight transport terms, the express bus system looked the best bet, realising what economists term a positive net present value of £1 to £5million. By comparison, a 7.5-mile rail system, which would cost about £65 million and would include both north-south and east-west legs, was calculated as having a *negative* net present value of between £25 and £31 million. However, the report did say that the express buses were unlikely to have much effect on employment in Docklands,

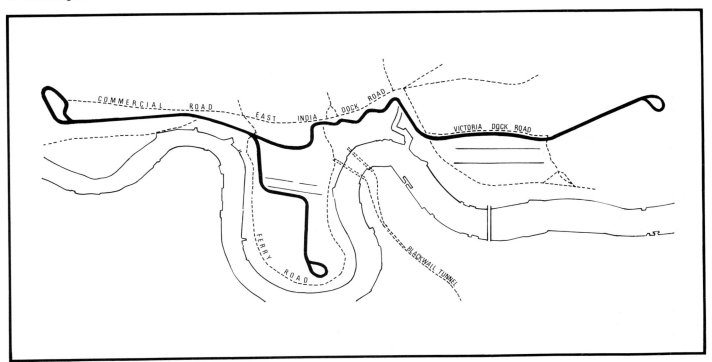

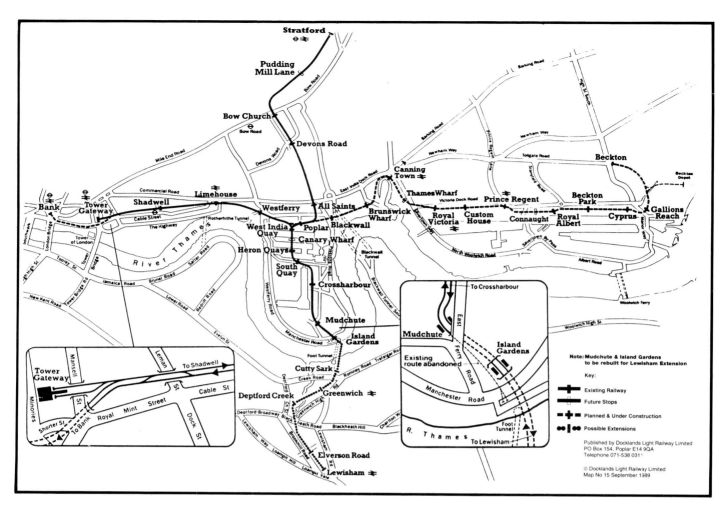

Published by Docklands Light Railway Limited
PO Box 154, Poplar E14 9QA
Telephone 071-538 0311

© Docklands Light Railway Limited
Map No 15 September 1989

Above:
Map of the Docklands Light Railway (DLR). The initial system is shown in a heavy black line.

Left:
The London & Blackwall Railway route used by the DLR in the Limehouse area. This is the future site of the West Ferry station (marked 'stn' on the bridge abutment) in September 1983. *John Glover*

whereas it was thought that the light rail system could act as a stimulant for development, and that this could outweigh its poor showing in transport terms.

Thus the LDDC and the GLC came to throw their weight behind the idea of a light railway. They were a pair of strange bedfellows: the LDDC was a creation of the Conservative government chaired by a prominent capitalist, Nigel Broakes, while the Labour GLC was led by left-winger Ken Livingstone. It was something of a triumph that these two very different bodies came together in backing the DLR idea, as for some time the GLC's preferred transport strategy for Docklands had been the Jubilee Line extension. As the London Underground chief of the time, Tony Ridley, tells the story, the joint push for the DLR came about thanks to the vision of Dave Wetzel, then the GLC transport chair.

Wetzel was a colourful figure whose political views were what he himself termed 'anarcho-syndicalist', and whose

gastronomic tastes were said to embrace a preference for brown sauce with his apple pie. But perhaps more importantly, from the point of view of this history, he was a man who held the good of London's public transport system close to his heart. Transport planners managed to convince him that Jubilee was just too expensive for the Government to accept and that inexpensive light rail was the only hope for Docklands — and Wetzel did the important job of selling this notion to the Labour GLC.

Political consensus is always a big help in getting a public infrastructure project off the ground, and in this case events moved very quickly. Michael Heseltine, who at the time was the Government minister with responsibility for the inner cities, gave the go-ahead for the construction of a light rail system in the Docklands in October 1982, just four months after the joint LDDC/GLC report was produced. It was an act of supreme political faith in the Docklands — and of faith in the ability of railways to stimulate development — by a Government generally regarded as antipathetic to the rail mode. The Government said the railway was not to cost more than £77 million (the £65 million estimated cost in the report of a north-south plus east-west railway, adjusted to take account of inflation during construction), and was to be open in 1987.

Final routes selected
Money was to be funnelled to the project through the LDDC and the GLC, with LT

deputed to prepare the Parliamentary plans. The aim was to have the plans submitted to Parliament in November 1983, with Parliamentary authority to build the line coming the following spring and tenders being let then — all to meet the very tight timescale of being open in 1987.

As 1983 progressed, the routes were firmed up. At the northern end, Mile End was replaced by Stratford as the favoured terminus, made possible by agreement with BR concerning the release of a trackbed into Stratford. The choice of Stratford made interchange with BR services from a wide area of East Anglia possible, as well as the Central Line of the Underground.

At the same time, the LDDC was insisting on elevation of the railway on the Isle of Dogs, to make it highly visible and a symbol of the regeneration of the area. As the rest of the route was planned round old railway rights of way, these two changes made complete segregation from road traffic — and thus automation — possible.

The LDDC, which would be part-owner of the new railway, was very keen on the idea of automation, as it would reinforce the image of being on the cutting edge of technology that the Corporation was trying to instil in its efforts to stimulate development in the derelict docks. Manufacturers of automated systems abroad were assessed: planners looked at the Matra system used on the world's first automated metro in Lille, France; the UTDC alternative with linear induction motors as

used on the Skytrain in Vancouver on the western coast of Canada; and Westinghouse, a well-established manufacturer of automated peoplemovers for airports in the US.

The western terminus of the line was set at Minories, at the east end of BR's Fenchurch Street station. A direct link with the Underground — either at Tower Hill or Aldgate East — had been the preferred option, but the Minories site (later to be called Tower Gateway) was chosen to keep within the £77 million ceiling. BR agreed to give up two of its four tracks on the approach to Fenchurch Street (a decision it would later come to regret, as an increase in commuter traffic from southeast Essex has made this a serious bottleneck on the London, Tilbury & Southend line) and by this means the new light railway would reach BR's Stepney East station (now named Limehouse). From there, it would swing south on an abandoned railway viaduct

7

towards the Isle of Dogs. At a junction at the north end of the Isle of Dogs the line would split, with the northward section running on an old rail solum towards Stratford, and the southward section performing its high-visibility role on a new steel and concrete viaduct over the old West India Docks. A terminus at the southern end of the peninsula was to be reached using another old railway viaduct through Millwall Park.

Decisions were taken at this time that were to cause headaches later on when the railway proved so successful and had to be expanded. Poplar was chosen as the site for the depot, as it was central to the system and it seemed unlikely that there would be any extensions built. With the expansion of the system and the train fleet, the depot has proved to be cramped. It certainly would have made life easier for today's engineers if another, larger site investigated in the initial planning stage — the old Devons Road steam shed near Stratford — had been chosen in preference to Poplar!

In planning the new construction in the Isle of Dogs, it was thought unlikely that

Below:
At its western end, the DLR runs parallel to the British Rail Fenchurch Street line. This photograph, taken from the platform of the disused Leman Street station about one-third of a mile from Tower Gateway, shows sitework for the new viaduct. *DLR.*

there would ever be any need to go to two-car trains on this section, and the whole railway — platform length, viaduct strength and so on — was based on this premise. Modifications have since had to be made to cope with longer trains.

Turnkey contract

At the outset, it was thought that a number of separate contracts would be let, with LT's DLR team overseeing the builders and fitting the elements of the complete railway together. By the spring of 1984, tenders had been invited for the vehicles, and the DLR team was ready to send out tender information for the civil engineering work. At the eleventh hour, instructions were received from the Government that the tender documents for the civil work were not to be sent out. Instead, the Government had decided that a novel form of contract — known as design-and-build — would be used for the new railway. Industry would be asked to put in bids to build the complete railway: civil works, trains, signalling and all. The winning bidder would have responsibility for handing the finished railway over to LT by the contract date and within budget.

Thus the new urban railway was treated much as an item in a supermarket: the finished product was to be bought off the shelf, and if there were any complaints about quality, the purchaser could write to the manufacturer. Unlike conventional railway projects, LT would have little say in what went on during the construction

phase. Since the building of the DLR, the idea has been taken a logical stage further on other projects, to include not only design and building, but also operation and maintenance (Dbom): the Manchester Metrolink light rail project is an example of a scheme being realised on this basis. Compared to a simple design-and-build contract like the DLR, Dbom has the merit that the builder has to live with the consequences in the event of mistakes being made in the construction process.

Adopting what was then a revolutionary design-and-build contract made the DLR work a different ball game; most importantly, it made the £77 million cost ceiling look attainable. 'The DLR's life was on the line right up until the contract was signed, as in January 1984 it didn't look like we would get within the £77 million', remembers an insider at LT at the time. 'The design-and-build contract made it possible, so it must be considered a good move.'

Proposals were invited from three teams: Metro-Cammell of Birmingham, with UTDC, Hawker Siddeley and Balfour Beatty; traction equipment manufacturers GEC with civil engineers Mowlem; and a German consortium comprising Siemens, AEG and Duewag.

In August 1984, GEC-Mowlem was awarded the design-and-build contract, with the remit to have the system operating within three years. For the winning consortium, competition against the other bidders was replaced by a race against time: GEC-Mowlem was now obliged to

complete a new automated railway, the first of its type in Britain, within a timeframe quite unlike any ever attempted before in this country for projects of a similar magnitude and technical sophistication. That the feat was accomplished, within budget and only one month late, is a considerable tribute to those involved.

Right:
Tower Gateway station under construction. Tony Ridley, London Underground Managing Director at the time the DLR was planned, describes the western terminus of the DLR as 'abominable' but freely admits responsibility: 'If we'd loaded that project [the DLR] with the cost of a proper interchange, it would not have happened'.

Left and below:
Foundations in a muddy trench *(left)* **give rise to reinforced concrete pillars** *(below)* **which turn** *(bottom)* **into the elegant delta junction at Poplar.**
DLR/Barfab Reinforcements/M. F. Haddon

Right:
The final span is placed in the viaduct linking Heron Quays (background) and Canary Wharf (camera position) in the West India Docks. *DLR*

Far right:
The viaduct leaps over water and joins Heron Quays (middle background) and Canary Wharf (with warehouses, in background). *DLR*

RAILWAY TAKES SHAPE

Above:
Old warehouses dominate Canary Wharf as it was during construction of the DLR. *DLR*

Right:
A floating crane completes the viaduct. *DLR*

2: THE RACE AGAINST TIME

AS GEC-Mowlem took up work on the Docklands contract in earnest, it found it had a war to wage on three fronts. First, there were the very tight cost constraints; second, the three-year timeframe from contract to opening ('suicidally tight' one GEC executive has been quoted as saying); and third, many new technologies would be tried out for the first time in an urban transit environment on the DLR.

The decision to go for a light railway helped considerably in keeping the costs down. The system would be physically separate from the BR network, and thus it was not necessary to meet conventional railway end loading requirements and the trains could be lighter: tare weight of a DLR unit is approximately 39 tonnes. Light trains

meant light — and thus cheap — structures. The running rails are 71% of the weight of normal BR rails.

Route planning and construction was simplified as the trains could climb steep grades (5% on the initial system, 6% on the Bank extension) and negotiate sharp curves (as tight as 40m, while 150m would be considered very tight on BR). As the DLR's budget ruled out large-scale compulsory land purchase, the new line would have to twist and bend its way from one piece of LDDC land to another down the Isle of Dogs.

The experience and expertise of the Mowlem company were called on to execute the civil works, while subcontracts were let to Brown & Root Vickers for the workshop and maintenance facility at Poplar and to Grant Lyon Eagre for the trackwork. The LDDC had been keen on a third rail power supply system as it would be less visually obtrusive than overhead,

and a novel (for Britain) underside contact aluminium rail was supplied by Brecknell Willis.

Meanwhile, the GEC half of the consortium was grappling with the mechanical and electrical side of the contract. Trains were ordered from Linke Hoffmann Busch (LHB), which had an articulation system that could cope with the tight curves in Docklands.

At prices getting on for £1 million apiece, the trains were one of the most expensive pieces of kit for the new railway — and thus

Below:
Limehouse station under construction, August 1986. The Victorian railway viaduct that was reused here was built with a lime mortar that allowed a certain amount of movement, enabling it to stand up to the Blitz and years of neglect. *M. F. Haddon*

one giving large scope for paring costs in the effort to keep to a tight budget. The 'optional extras' were declined — resulting in a fairly basic light rail vehicle — and the number of trains ordered was kept to a bare minimum. Nine trains would be needed to run the 7.5min headways in the specification, plus two maintenance spares, giving a total fleet of 11.

A new control system
Automation was to give the contractors some of their biggest headaches. True, automation was not new, as the Lille and Vancouver systems had no drivers, and several other metros — including the Victoria Line in London — had automatic operation while retaining drivers for residual duties such as door operation. But the

Above:
The DLR claimed two of the four BR tracks in the approach to Fenchurch Street. An Essex-bound multiple-unit passes the site of Shadwell station on 16 August 1986. *M. F. Haddon*

Left:
Bow Road station on the DLR's Stratford line nears completion. *M. F. Haddon*

Below:
Diagram showing the underside contact rail used on the DLR.
This design avoids the problems with snow and ice that plague the topside contact third rails on BR. *DLR*

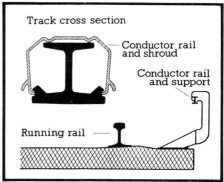

Track cross section
Conductor rail and shroud
Conductor rail and support
Running rail

Development takes off
For years, property developers had been wary of the Docklands, with its reputation for rotting industry, outdated infrastructure and mean streets. Michael Heseltine's 1982 announcement giving the go-ahead for the light railway did not convince them that the Government was serious about revitalising the area. Royal Assent to the Act authorising the DLR in 1984 multiplied the enquiries about development to the LDDC some ten-fold, but it was only when the DLR's concrete piers actually started appearing out of the ground that land prices really took off.

The development that was to put Docklands into a different league germinated in 1985, when the original Canary Wharf developers suggested 10 million sq ft of office space (equivalent to one-fifth of the space in the City of London), rather than the 400,000sq ft then envisaged by the LDDC.

In an ambitious move, the Canadian property company, Olympia & York, took over the Canary Wharf development in July 1987. O&Y is very big in North America, owning large chunks of Manhattan, but this was its first development in the UK. It was a stylish entry: the 800ft tower at Canary Wharf is the tallest building in the country, and the complex has a projected employment level of 50,000 by 1996. The first tenants were due to move in during 1991.

Other developments on the Isle of Dogs have taken off, and current forecasts are for an eventual 135,000 jobs there (the DLR was originally planned with 20,000 jobs in mind). Housing and leisure facilities are being built alongside the offices. The property slump that hit London in the late 1980s knocked the sheen off some of this, but did not alter the central fact that London's Docklands have been transformed.

Even before it opened, the DLR had accomplished one of its major tasks: the railway had pump-primed the Isle of Dogs property market and changed the image of the Docklands for ever.

Above:
The Olympia & York development at Canary Wharf towers over a BREL-built train at Heron Quays in January 1991.
David Bateman

particular systems adopted for Docklands had their first urban transit application there, and this gave rise to some problems.

The automatic train control system comprised two separate elements: automatic train protection (ATP) and automatic train operation (ATO). The ATP system prevents trains running into one another — on a conventional railway ATP will not allow trains to pass red signals (BR is currently installing its first ATP systems on the Chiltern and Great Western lines). The 'brain' behind the ATP on the DLR is solid state interlocking (SSI), a system that uses computer logic (rather than cumbersome electro-mechanical relays) to ensure two trains cannot enter the same section of track. A signal is transmitted along the rails while it is safe for a train to enter a block. This signal is picked up by coils on the leading bogie and the train is given permission to proceed. Its absence is taken as a train stop command, the power to the traction motors is shut off and the emergency brakes are applied.

The ATP also guards against overspeeding. Passengers on a DLR train can see the 'wiggly wires' that prevent overspeeding in the 4ft between the rails. Every so often, the wires cross: each crossing point is detected by a coil on the train, and if the train passes over successive crosses in too short a time, the emergency brakes are applied. This system works when trains are being driven manually (unless in the slow-speed 'shunt' mode) as well as automatically.

The ATO system communicates with the train via data docking links (DDLs), the wooden boxes that can be seen in the four-foot at stations. The DDL talks to an on-board computer, which has stored in its memory a series of speed/distance profiles. Each profile defines how fast a train should be travelling at any point between stations and the ATO computer makes the train follow this profile by applying power, letting the train coast or applying the brakes. The DDL will tell the train to use either a maximum speed mode (if it is running behind time) or an energy conservation mode in normal circumstances.

The ATO instructions come from a central computer at Poplar, which

Left:
A 'coffin': this wooden box houses a data docking link for the ATO system. 'Wiggly wires' for the ATP can be seen in the middle of the four-foot. *Brian Morrison*

authorises trains to leave stations, sets appropriate routes and so on. A system known as automatic train supervision (ATS) holds the train timetable and compares it with reality, while an automatic vehicle regulation (AVR) program tries to make reality conform with the timetable by holding trains and choosing between the coasting and high speed profiles on the trains.

First time on an urban system
The train control system involved various elements which had not been used before on an urban railway. SSI was a collaborative development by GEC-General Signal, Westinghouse Brake & Signal and British Rail which put Britain in the forefront of this form of signalling and, although now well-proven, had only been used on lines with relatively modest traffic flows when applied to the DLR.

The ATS system used the Trafficmaster 2 computer developed by GEC's signalling partner, General Railway Signalling of the USA, which had been designed with simple freight systems in mind. It required some adaptation to fit the DLR.

Making the individual systems mesh together and writing the digital reams of bespoke software needed to operate them took a huge effort, but one that was accomplished within the necessary timeframe.

The railway is completed
As the beautiful summer of 1987 arrived, the new railway was close to being ready. It was handed over to its new owners, the LDDC and London Regional Transport (the latter having taken over the share of the GLC in the DLR when responsibility for transport was taken away from that body in June 1984) 32 months after work started and just two weeks late on the initial programme.

GEC-Mowlem was proud of its creation: trials without passengers showed the system could perform to the specification, running at 7.5min headways. Whether or not the consortium made any money out of it was a moot point: the final price paid was reportedly £60.5 million (£43.5 million for civil work and £17 million for electrical and mechanical), up £2 million on the £58.5 million agreed with the consortium at the outset. (The £77 million ceiling set by the Government was to cover everything involved with the railway: consultants' fees, land acquisition and so on, as well as the turnkey contract fee.) At best, the consortium broke even on the deal: it was regarded as a good shopwindow for obtaining future light rail work in the UK.

By midsummer 1987, a final polish was being given to the shopwindow. All was made ready for the Royal opening, scheduled to be undertaken by Her Majesty The Queen on 30 July. The gigantic task had been accomplished: London now had a new high-tech railway, built in a phenomenally short time at a quite remarkably low cost.

Below:
The pristine new railway: unit 09 crosses the West India docks in pre-opening trials. *John Mowlem & Co PLC.*

3: FROM ROYALTY TO REALITY

ON 30 July 1987, Her Majesty Queen Elizabeth II officially opened the Docklands Light Railway and rode in one of its trains. There were a couple of minor hitches on opening day: the train carrying the Queen had to be driven manually for a while, and there was a problem about opening the doors. The first problem originated because the Royal party arrived early, and the computer (no respecter of Royal privileges) was holding it for a couple of minutes until it fitted in with the timetable; railway staff decided to intervene to get things moving. The door problem occurred because a Royal bodyguard, in a bid to be out on the platform before the monarch, had gone for an emergency exit — the train thus made an emergency stop short of the data docking link and there was then a problem in opening the rest of the doors, as the train did not 'know' it was in a station.

Ironically, the hitches showed that the system was working correctly — but that did not stop the daily press from rubbishing the railway. Nor was there much mercy shown for the way in which the railway did not open the day after the Royal opening,

Above:
Royal train: Her Majesty The Queen in a bedecked unit 11, 30 July 1987. *DLR*

Left:
The monarch gets the same driver's-eye view that can be enjoyed by her subjects as unit 11 leaves the delta junction en-route to Poplar station. *Brian Morrison*

as originally intended, but a month later. The DLR decided, sensibly enough, that it wanted two weeks' problem-free trial running before opening to the public, and minor glitches had prevented the attainment of that goal by the end of July. The important point was not that the DLR was a couple of weeks late, but that the complete new railway had been constructed in just three years. When the public opening did take place, on Bank Holiday Monday, 31 August 1987, there was immense interest and huge crowds swamped the DLR. As many as 40,000 people may have ridden the trains on the first day.

The railway filled a gap in the local public transport infrastructure and soon attracted

The GEC-Mowlem Railway Group was main contractor for the
first phase of the Docklands Light Railway.

GEC ALSTHOM

Transport Division

Two separate contracts were issued: one for upgrading the initial system was given to the system's builders, GEC-Mowlem, and the other, for construction of the tunnel to Bank, went out to tender and was won by the Edmund Nuttall company. The contracts were signed on 18 July 1987, within hours of agreement with Olympia & York, the new owners of the Canary Wharf development, on the financing of the City extension.

The instruction to GEC-Mowlem was a design-and-build contract similar to the one for the initial system, with the consortium to buy more trains, upgrade the computer and so forth to provide the required extra capacity. Timing of the contract fell between two stools: it was not early enough to get anything done before the opening of the initial system, and yet too soon to see if

regular heavy loadings. Market surveys have shown that the pre-1981 inhabitants of Docklands regard the DLR as being the most valuable improvement to the area that has been carried out by the LDDC.

Upgrading announced
Even before the first fare-paying passengers were carried, arrangements had been made to upgrade the DLR. With plans firming up for the huge office development at Canary Wharf, it was plain that the DLR as built would be unable to cope.

To make Canary Wharf attractive to the financial services industry, the developer was keen on extending the light railway into the heart of the City at Bank rather than having it terminate on the fringes at Tower Gateway. Furthermore, it seemed willing to back that wish with some investment funds. There was talk of delaying the opening of the rest of the system to await the completion of a tunnel to Bank: in the event it was decided to press on with the initial system, opening the Bank extension later.

A Parliamentary Bill was deposited for an extension to Bank in November 1985, receiving Royal Assent in December 1986.

Below:
Stand-by royal train. Unit 10 with Royal standard is seen at Stratford on 31 July 1987, the day when it had originally been hoped to open the DLR to the public. *R. J. Waterhouse*

the design-and-build idea had any flaws when it came to operating the system.

Problems appear

While the problems that attended the Royal opening were not really problems at all, some real ones set in soon enough. The beautiful summer of 1987 turned into a misty, damp autumn and winter. Something that was not apparent in the trial running then manifested itself: when the rails were greasy, the trains would overrun stations. A few metres beyond the data docking link, and a train would be 'lost'; the train captain would then have to set back in a time-consuming operation so that it could 'find' itself again. This problem was eventually solved by installing check loops in the four-foot, 30m before the data docking link, to warn the train it is approaching a DDL and finetuning the braking curve.

The ATO presented a more intractable problem. While the computer was fine at running the timetable when there were no passengers to complicate things, in service running matters were not quite so simple. An old lady might get stuck in the door at Bow Church, or a drunk might be causing problems at Limehouse. Whatever the cause, in the real world every so often trains will run late. The computer felt most comfortable handling perfection and would be constantly striving to return to the working timetable, holding trains that were ready to leave to let the late ones catch up. The problem became most acute at the delta junction at Poplar, where a problem on say the Stratford branch would start affecting services on the Tower Gateway leg — even though there was nothing wrong on the western line. If intervention by the control room became frequent, the fault buffers on the computer would fill up and it would say, in effect, 'if you think you can do this better than I can, you get on with it'.

Disillusonment set in. There were 2,100 applicants for the 42 train captain posts when they were first advertised before the railway opened, but after it had been open for a while the DLR had difficulty in retaining staff.

Who was to blame?

Just who was responsible for the operating problems became a subject of some acrimony. GEC-Mowlem would argue that it had met the specification — it was just that the spec was wrong. The DLR would counter that although, maybe, the letter of the spec had been met, it had not been met in spirit, and that some of the practical difficulties should have been anticipated.

There is probably an element of justice on both sides. The spec was not all it might have been: for instance, it specified a 15sec dwell time at stations, which is fine if you have no passengers, but wildly over-optimistic if there are more than a handful. On the other hand, there may have been some elements where workmanship could have been better; but how much is it fair to expect for the rock-bottom price for which the DLR was provided?

Then the DLR became a victim of its own success. It had done what it was intended to do: it had breathed life into the Docklands property market. As a result, rather than being the white elephant some had feared, it rapidly became too small for the job.

The practical difficulties of running the DLR were exacerbated by engineering work, as the railway had not even started running before work had begun on increasing its capacity in the Phase II upgrading works. Trying to run the railway while works teams were crawling all over it became a bit like trying to drive a mini, while at the same time turning it into a double-decker bus.

Top:
Unit 06 snakes down the Isle of Dogs with a capacity load on opening day, 31 August 1987. *Michael McGowan*

Above:
Unit 08 leaves Mudchute for Tower Gateway, wrong line, as a result of a points failure further south on 3 October 1987. *John C. Baker*

Below:
Bank Holiday crowds fill the platform at Stratford on the first day of DLR service. A Central Line train for Ruislip leaves at right. *Michael McGowan*

A DLR train skirting Millwall Park on the old Millwall Extension Railway single-track viaduct. In the background is Island Gardens station, and behind that the Royal Naval College/National Maritime Museum complex on the other side of the river in Greenwich. On top of the hill in the far background is the Old Royal Observatory. *DLR*

Above:
Diagram showing the DLR tunnel in relation to tube tunnels at Bank: not shown here is a proposed direct pedestrian link from the DLR to the Northern Line. This would go from the DLR inter-platform concourse, over the DLR eastbound platform tunnel and under the northbound Northern Line platform tunnel before emerging between the Northern Line platforms — an extremely tricky piece of tunnelling.
DLR

The growing railway:
artist's impression of the DLR station at Beckton Park on the Beckton extension.
DLR

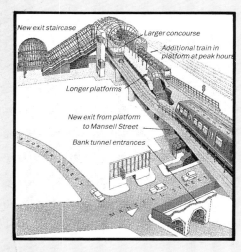

New exit staircase
Larger concourse
Additional train in platform at peak hours
Longer platforms
New exit from platform to Mansell Street
Bank tunnel entrances

Changes at Tower Gateway

Above:
A new exit from the eastern end of the platform to Mansell Street has been installed, plus extra stairs at the main entrance. *DLR*

Right:
Barriers separate the crowd flow at rush-hour. *David Bateman*

Below:
The new Westinghouse Cubic ticket machine, which (unlike the original Thorn EMI ticket machines at left) dispenses travelcards as well as ordinary tickets. This could become the standard machine for the whole network. *Brian Morrison*

RAILWAY

Making way for the Limehouse Link
Over the weekend 29-30 September 1990, the Victorian brick viaduct under the DLR to the east of Westferry station (*right*) was removed by Balfour Beatty and replaced by a steel and concrete girder bridge to facilitate building the (partly-submerged) new road from Wapping to the Isle of Dogs. 1,200

separate charges, each to be fired a few thousandths of a second before the neighbouring charge, were installed in the old viaduct and detonated at 07.30 on the Saturday (*above*).

Complicating the introduction of the new bridge was its asymmetrical design at the eastern end, as it included part of the complicated replacement for the simple delta junction at Poplar; the long side of the bridge would have to pass through the short side of the gap left by the demolition of the old viaduct. A set of computer-controlled hydraulically-powered bogies (similar to 'moon buggies') were used on the Saturday afternoon to manoeuvre the new bridge through the gap at an angle, then to reverse back into position (*above right*). The new bridge was ready for the start of services on the Monday morning (*right*) less than 48hrs after the demolition of the old viaduct. *All: DLR*

This page:
The DLR at Island Gardens, May 1989.
David Haydock

4: A MINI INTO A DOUBLE-DECKER BUS

AT the time the DLR was being planned, it was routed through what was then a wasteland of deserted wharves and abandoned buildings. It was hoped the new railway would stimulate development: new light industry units and low-rise offices were thought to be on the cards, but nothing of the scale of Canary Wharf ever featured in even the LDDC's wildest dreams.

Consequently, the system specifiers sought a carrying capacity that today seems ludicrously small. The performance specification sent out to the bidders for the turnkey contract for the initial system asked them to cater for maximum peak direction flows between Tower Hill and Island Gardens of 900 passengers/hr (pph), and between Stratford and Island Gardens of 800pph, giving total peak direction flows on the common Isle of Dogs route of 1,700pph (by comparison, a tube line can handle about 20,000pph). A 7.5min headway throughout the day from both Tower Gateway and Stratford was required, and a 10min headway during evenings and weekends. The specification did offer the caveat 'It is possible that the nature of future development in Docklands and the character of services offered by the DLR shall cause a significant change in these patterns. It is particularly important, therefore, that the proposed system retains sufficient flexibility of capacity and routeing to accommodate changes in demand, both overall and locally'. But it would surely be unfair to expect any supplier (especially one hamstrung by a tight cost ceiling) to have made adequate provision for what has happened.

Explosive development in the Isle of Dogs — catalysed by the presence of the railway — has meant that the DLR now regularly runs crushloaded. Surveys in the northbound direction at South Quay in the evening rush during January 1990 showed loadings of around 2,000pph — and that was only halfway up the Island, with peak loadings not reached until north of West India Quay! Looked at in one way, the DLR is an outstanding success, carrying almost 20% more passengers than the number for which it was designed just a couple of years after opening; on the other side of the coin, passengers are squeezed into every nook and cranny and inconvenienced as work

Above:

Upgrading for two-car trains: platform extensions can be clearly seen in this February 1990 view at West India Quay.
Brian Morrison

goes ahead at expanding the capacity of the system.

At the time the survey was taken at South Quay, Canary Wharf was the workplace of construction labourers rather than the 50,000 office workers projected for the development. At what rate the DLR's passenger levels will go on rising is anyone's guess — 15,000pph by 1993 has been suggested in some quarters.

Upgrading contract
The DLR's likely undercapacity was apparent even before its opening: hence the decision to contract GEC-Mowlem to upgrade the initial system at a price not much less than it cost to build in the first place. The essential requirement in the upgrading was for trains to run down the Isle of Dogs at 2min intervals — giving a 4min headway on both the City and Stratford lines. Some, at least, of these trains would be formed with two units, rather than the one used for the first few years of operation.

Thus extra trains were needed: GEC-Mowlem contracted BREL to build 10 new trains under licence from LHB, with the intention of acquiring more later (although that intention was never realised, as the

DLR ordered more trains directly from BN of Belgium).

Structural work
The upgraded specification meant some structural work was required. The steel and concrete viaducts on the DLR had been built to bear just one unit, and an ingenious piston device (as shown in the diagram) has been inserted in them to spread the load of two-unit trains and thus avoid any need to rebuild the structure.

The platforms on the DLR were built to accommodate a single articulated unit, and needed lengthening to hold two units. This work was finished by the end of 1990 at all but Mudchute and Island Gardens stations at the south end of the Isle of Dogs: here there was no land available to lengthen the platforms. Some two-car trains will turn round at Canary Wharf, and others at Crossharbour, with the two southern stations being served by single-car services. Turnback sidings to facilitate this method of working have been installed at both Canary Wharf, where a new station has been built to serve the office tower and Crossharbour. A loop has been built at Pudding Mill Lane, on the single-track stretch of line between Bow Church and Stratford, to increase track capacity.

The initial system was built with just one substation to feed the third rail; three additional substations have been built under the upgrading. With four substations, one can go out of commission and the railway can still keep running.

Upgraded control system

To handle the more frequent services and to knock the bugs out that had appeared when the DLR began service running, extensive modifications have been made to the GEC-General Signal control system. Improvements have been made to the interface between the various aspects of the system, so time would not be wasted holding trains unnecessarily in order to conform to some notional timetable.

By the end of 1990, the computer showed it could deliver what was required of it: tests one Saturday in December showed a headway of less than 1min 40secs could be maintained on the Isle of Dogs line. The Seltrac moving block system which will replace it in 1992 should be able to accommodate trains running at a 1min headway, and will give the leeway to recover quickly from any operational setbacks.

Below:
Chart showing how daily traffic on the DLR has grown steadily: summer peaks denote the new railway's drawing power for curious tourists. Traffic has slipped when the service has been rendered unreliable by engineering work: system upgrading started in earnest in the spring of 1989, work on the new interchange at Poplar started that autumn, and ATS2, a control system upgrading, came in with some teething problems in early 1990.
DLR

Service disruption

Turning the mini into a double-decker bus has been an expensive and disruptive operation. The DLR has been closed in the late evenings and weekends for much of its life to allow the engineers free rein, with a bus service put on instead. The GEC-Mowlem team has had possession of the railway from 22.00 to 04.00 Mondays to Thursdays, and from 22.00 on Fridays to 04.00 on Mondays — working such anti-social hours implies high labour costs. Some weekends have been very hectic, with say a control system modification being tried out on one stretch of track, while a new train was tried out on another.

The consortium prided itself on handing back the railway each Monday morning in working order: on occasion, it has been necessary to begin the week with manual driving and service reliability has not always been all it might have been, but service was never suspended completely on account of the engineering work. It is an operation without parallel elsewhere in the world: the Lille metro, for instance, was closed for six weeks for the installation of a new control centre prior to opening of a second line.

People-moving muscle

The two-vehicle trains on a 2min headway now planned for the Isle of Dogs should be able to handle 12,000pph. The Seltrac moving block system should be able to squeeze the headway down further if necessary, and with some more

modifications the DLR would be able to handle three-car trains. Trains of this length running at 2min headways would take the DLR's capacity up to 18,000pph — multiplying by more than 10 the maximum flows predicted in the original specification, and giving the light railway almost as much people-carrying power as a tube.

Below:
The viaducts on the DLR were designed for single-car trains. To spread the load of two-car trains, shock transmission units as shown here have been installed at rail level in the expansion joints between continuous seven-span deck units. Increased traction and braking loading on one unit is thus shared with adjacent spans, sufficiently to require no pier or foundation strengthening.
Colebrand

Bottom:
**Track diagram showing Bank and Beckton extensions, Canary Wharf layout, new Crossharbour siding and Pudding Mill Lane loop
— a station should open in this loop by the end of 1995. Also shown on the Stratford branch is the site of Carmen Street station, strongly supported by the London Borough of Tower Hamlets but which is difficult to justify financially. Planned quadrupling at West India Quay and proposed changes at Leman Street junction and Stratford station will change the appearance of this diagram.** *DLR*

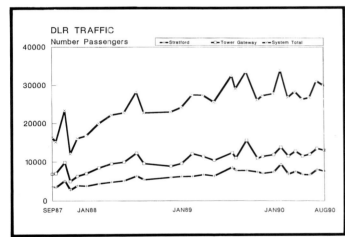

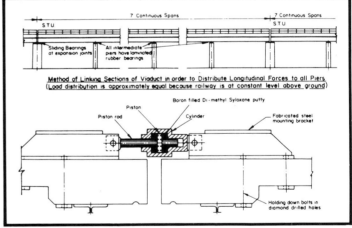

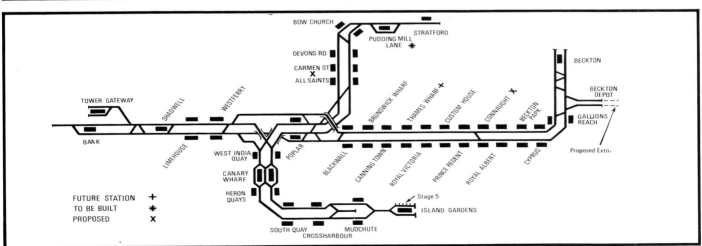

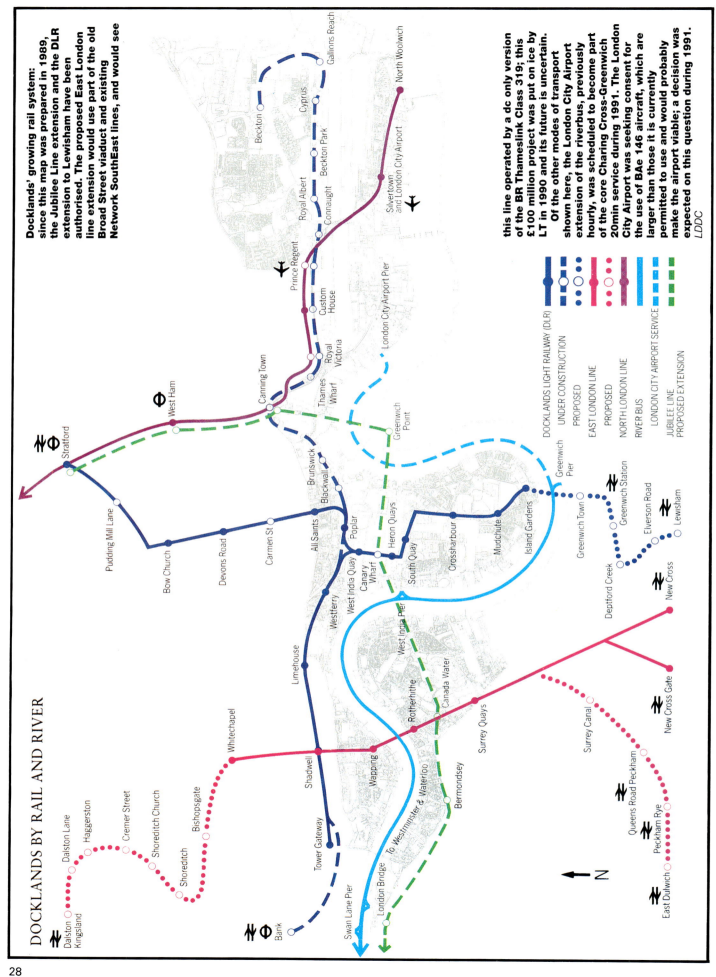

DOCKLANDS BY RAIL AND RIVER

Docklands' growing rail system: since this map was prepared in 1989, the Jubilee Line extension and the DLR extension to Lewisham have been authorised. The proposed East London line extension would use part of the old Broad Street viaduct and existing Network SouthEast lines, and would see

this line operated by a dc only version of the BR Thameslink Class 319; this £100 million project was put on ice by LT in 1990 and its future is uncertain.

Of the other modes of transport shown here, the London City Airport extension of the riverbus, previously hourly, was scheduled to become part of the core Charing Cross-Greenwich 20min service during 1991. The London City Airport was seeking consent for the use of BAe 146 aircraft, which are larger than those it is currently permitted to use and would probably make the airport viable; a decision was expected on this question during 1991.

LDDC

DOCKLANDS LIGHT RAILWAY (DLR)
UNDER CONSTRUCTION
PROPOSED
EAST LONDON LINE
PROPOSED
NORTH LONDON LINE
RIVER BUS
LONDON CITY AIRPORT SERVICE
JUBILEE LINE
PROPOSED EXTENSION

Left:
Route map for the DLR once the Beckton extension is in operation: while the northern leg of the delta junction at Poplar has not been in regular use with the initial system service pattern, this route in the modified junction will be used by Beckton trains. *DLR*

Below:
Poplar Depot. *Brian Morrison*

5: A NEW SIGNALLING SYSTEM

AS the Docklands Light Railway has grown, so has the complexity of its operations. The GEC-General Signal signalling system was designed for a 7.5min headway service on the simple initial railway, and — leaving aside the problems that were experienced with this system — the DLR management thought that with the coming of the Beckton extension, Canary Wharf and the requirement for a 2min headway on the Isle of Dogs, it was appropriate to reconsider the railway's signalling system.

Accordingly, the two major British signalling companies —GEC and Westinghouse — were asked for ideas about how to approach this problem, and the DLR paid for each to compile a design brief on how best to meet the changed signalling requirements of the growing railway. GEC put forward a plan based on the Seltrac system of Alcatel, a Canadian company which — following a series of mergers in the international railway manufacturing industry — is now one of GEC's corporate relations, while Westinghouse put forward a modified version of the system it had developed for the Singapore metro. The upshot of this exercise was that Seltrac was chosen to be

Below:
Diagram showing the concept of the moving block signalling system.

the new signalling system for the DLR and in May 1990 Alcatel — now assuming the lead role — was awarded a £26.4 million contract. GEC was subcontracted to fit out Beckton depot with the new signalling system.

Moving block
Alcatel's Seltrac is a development of a system designed by Standard Elektrik Lorenz (SEL) which had its first urban application on Line 4 of the Berlin U-Bahn, and more recently was used on the tunnel section of the Düsseldorf light rail system.

Seltrac employs a concept known as moving block; this is fundamentally different to the form of signalling with which most British railway staff are familiar. Conventional railway signalling is based on sections, or blocks of track, which are only allowed to be occupied by one train at a time. Latterly, occupation of a block has been detected by track circuits — low voltage current passed through the running rail which turns the signal behind to red when the axles of a train in the section complete the electrical circuit. While the original signalling on the DLR has all the sophistication of an automated system and has no lineside signals, its safety protection still rests on the fixed block system.

With a moving block system, instead of moving from fixed block to fixed block, trains can come right up behind one

another and make maximum use of the track space as vehicles on a road do— except that there is no danger of collision as there is on a road, as each train carries its own invisible envelope of space (a moving block) which the system ensures cannot be infringed by another train. Moving block has been used overseas for some time — it is, for instance, employed on the Lille metro. Alcatel's Seltrac moving block system has been used on the Skytrain in Vancouver, a city in which Canary Wharf developer Olympia & York has large land holdings, and on the Scarborough light rail system in O&Y's home town, Toronto.

Why moving block?
With the modified GEC-General Signal system achieving headways of less than 1min 40sec, it is worthwhile asking why the DLR is spending over £26 million on another system, when the busiest service envisaged involves 2min headways. Critics of the decision to purchase Seltrac point out that peak frequency on the Scarborough line is 2min 40sec and on the Skytrain 3min, and furthermore these are straight end-to-end lines, as opposed to the DLR's complex layout.

DLR Managing Director John Bygate admits that the 1min headways claimed for Seltrac are a manufacturer's puff and of limited significance on a heavily-used railway where the time taken by passengers

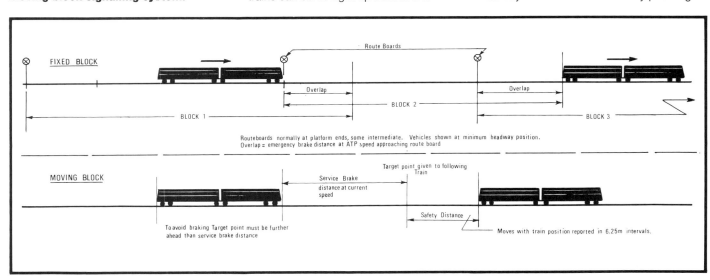

to get in and out of trains makes operation at such a headway impractical. However, he claims that Seltrac will be invaluable in making the DLR run smoothly, especially at the complex junctions at Poplar.

Here, the present delta junction between City, Isle of Dogs and Stratford branches will be joined 100m or so away by the junction between the Beckton and Stratford lines. A busy service will operate over all these routes and the potential for jams at the junctions is significant. Bygate claims that the Seltrac system will present the trains for procession through the junctions in a more orderly fashion than would be possible with the GEC-General Signal system, which was designed with a more simple railway in mind. The fact that Seltrac's former applications have been on straight end-to-end lines does not affect the

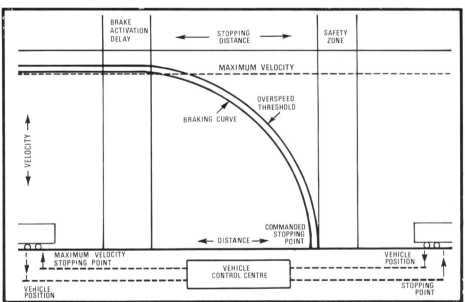

ability of the system to have trains in the right place at the right time for getting through the junctions quickly.

Bygate feels that much of the concern over the adoption of the new system stems from railway staff schooled in track circuits who are having difficulty in making the 'mental jump' to moving block — but that once that hurdle is cleared, Seltrac will be seen to be worthwhile.

How it works

With the Seltrac system, information is passed between the trains and the computer by inductive loop cables between the running rails. These cables are transposed at 25m intervals, with on-train sensors detecting the crossovers and comparing them from the train's axles, to give a precise indication of a train's location. The axle revolution counting starts afresh at each cable transposition, to prevent cumulative error over the train's location as a result of worn wheels.

There are three levels of computer. The top level provides the automatic train supervision function: it decides which train should have priority at a junction, what time trains should leave to conform to the timetable and so on — in short, the control centre's job on a traditional railway.

At the next level is the vehicle control centre (VCC) mini-computer, which performs the safety functions done by solid state interlocking in the original system, providing the automatic train protection and controlling the point interlockings. The role of the computer at this level is roughly analogous to that of the signalman on a traditional railway. The VCC receives location, speed, and direction of travel data from each train; it transmits back an updated safe stopping point (the boundary of the moving block), the maximum speed up to that point, and any required braking to stay within the speed profile on the gradient in the area where the train is located. This operation is performed more than 70 times each minute.

The third level computer, the VOBC (vehicle on-board computer), is on the trains and has a role akin to that of a driver. The VOBC takes the information from the two higher levels to make the train conform to the specifications they send out. It computes the braking curve for its particular train and carries out acceleration or deceleration as necessary, and also passes back its location position to the central computers.

The changeover

Seltrac will be the only control system installed on the Beckton extension; on the rest of the system it will be installed on top of the original system, lying dormant until the time comes for the changeover. Trains will not be dual-equipped: the P86, P89 and B90 stock run with the original equipment, while the B92 trains (the first of which is due to arrive in the spring of 1992) will be compatible only with Seltrac. (Further information on the different types of trains in use on the DLR follows in the next chapter.)

In the summer of 1992, trials and familiarisation exercises will be carried out with Seltrac on the Beckton line prior to public opening. During weekends in the autumn, it will be tried on the original part of the railway. When the DLR is confident Seltrac works on the original railway, a 'D-Day' weekend will occur: B92 trains that have been based at Beckton for the trials will swop over with the older stock at Poplar, and the railway will open on the Monday morning Seltrac-operated for the first time, with the B92s also making their public debut.

On 'D-Day', the P86 trains that will have been confined to working Stratford and Tower Gateway trains since the opening of the Bank tunnel, will be put in store. Meanwhile, engineering staff will set to with the P89s and B90s at Beckton, converting them to the Alcatel system.

A couple of months after Seltrac has come in on the initial system, it will be brought into public service on the Beckton extension.

This delicate operation will have to be planned meticulously if it is to succeed. It requires two fleets of trains, one unused and ready to take over from the other on 'D-Day'; the displaced fleet then has to be rapidly converted for the Beckton opening. While public service to Beckton is planned to take place before the end of 1992, conversion work will extend into the following year and the full 80-train strength will not be reached until the spring of 1993.

6: A FAST-GROWING FLEET

THE Docklands Light Railway is operated by a fleet of sleek modern vehicles similar to those found on light rail systems on the Continent. As the winner of the turnkey contract for supplying the complete initial railway, choice of manufacturer for the original batch of trains was down to GEC-Mowlem. The consortium turned to a firm well-versed in LRV construction: Linke Hoffman Busch (LHB) of Salzgitter, Germany.

Eleven two-car articulated vehicles were deemed sufficient to meet the turnkey contract specification requirements, and these LHB-built trains are numbered in a series 01 to 11 and known as P86 stock ('P' for Poplar depot, built in 1986).

The 28m-long trains are of steel construction, with four sets of bus-type inward opening doors on each side. Seating is mainly in bays of four, with some transverse seating over the centre bogie; there are 84 seats altogether. A Temperature Ltd heating system has been installed.

GEC traction equipment powers the trains: they have a beefy power-to-weight ratio of 10.1kW/tonne (by comparison, a BR Class 302 electric multiple-unit has a ratio of less than 4kW/tonne). The outer bogies in each vehicle are motored, with one frame-mounted equipment driving both bogies through right-angle drives. Control of the direct current traction equipment is by a microprocesser-controlled thyristor chopper incorporating gate turn off (GTO) thyristors.

Braking blends electric brakes with mechanical brakes: there is one disc on each axle. The electric brakes in the 'P' stock are rheostatic, which means the energy generated by the traction motors to slow the train is dissipated in resistors. These were chosen in preference to electrodynamic regenerating brakes, which return energy to the supply rail, as such brakes require another train to be

Above right:
The first train of all: Unit 01, Poplar Depot, September 1986. *Brian Morrison*

Right:
Inside P86 unit 03 soon after delivery. *Brian Morrison*

Left:
Arrival of the first BREL-built unit at Poplar, delivered in halves by road. *DLR*

accelerating nearby to work effectively — and at the train frequencies planned when the DLR was being built, it seemed unlikely that such a condition could be met all the time. Disc brakes and actuators were supplied by Lucas Girling, brake controls by Davies and Metcalfe, and brake cylinders by SAB.

The P86s have Scharfenberg automatic couplers, but these can only be used for shunting moves and the trains cannot be operated in multiple.

Vehicles 01-11 were built at Salzgitter; while it was originally planned that they would be fitted out at the Metro-Cammell works at Birmingham, in the event this did not happen and the GEC equipment was sent to Germany for fitting there. The trains were shipped via Hamburg and King's Lynn, arriving from the East Anglian port in halves by road; the first vehicle arrived on 7 August 1986.

Top-up order

As the Docklands area started to take off as a new centre of office employment, it became clear that extra capacity would be needed on the DLR. Thus as part of the 'upgrading' contract awarded to GEC-Mowlem in 1987, a further 10 trains were

ordered. This time round, the trains were built by BREL in York to the same design as the LHB vehicles. Known as P89 stock, the BREL vehicles are numbered 12-21.

P86 and P89 vehicles have the same appearance, but a number of changes have been made in the specification. The materials used in the interior of the P89s (phenolic resin rather than glass-reinforced epoxy resin) meet more rigorous fire-resistance standards and, in the wake of the King's Cross disaster, it has been decided that the P86s (which were ordered in a period when tunnel operation was not envisaged on the DLR) will not be used in the tunnel to Bank. They will be confined to Stratford and Tower Gateway services until the GEC-General Signal control system is retired in 1992, and then put into store.

The P89s were delivered with liquid crystal dot matrix destination signs at each end, while the P86s had roller blinds. These blinds could be operated by the train captain from a switch in the centre of the train and an ingenious design allowed the destination to appear both inside and outside the train; the problem with them was a tendency to tear. As a result, four-sided drums (with a destination on each side) were fitted below the original blinds as

a temporary expedient; these necessitated the train captain going from one end to the other to turn the drums over at each turnround, a procedure which could be tiresome in rush-hour crowds. These drawbacks have resulted in LCD signs being retrofitted to the old stock. The LCDs can be operated from one central point in the train.

One important modification is slated for the P89s. The bus-type doors on the 'P' stock have long been a source of frustration: their inward opening action is a nuisance on crowded trains as they can hit standing passengers, and they have been unreliable in service. For these reasons, the P89s are being retrofitted with conventional sliding doors. As the 'P' stock was designed to come close to the platform edge, plug doors which slide along the exterior of the car (as used on the new 'B' stock) were not feasible, and the new doors will slide in pockets within the car, as they do on conventional tube trains.

'B' stock

The DLR had an option with GEC to purchase 10 more P89s to cater for further traffic growth on the initial system. When the go-ahead was given for extension of the DLR to Beckton, it was apparent that yet more rolling stock would be needed to operate the new stretch of railway, so the option for 10 more vehicles was cancelled and the two orders rolled together. In total, 44 new trains were required: 34 for Beckton and 10 extras for the initial system.

While the 'P' stock had been ordered as part of the design-and-build contracts let for the construction of the initial system and its subsequent upgrading, the new stock was put out to tender by the DLR in the conventional way. The new stock has been dubbed 'B', for Beckton; the new depot being built on the Beckton extension will become the chief maintenance centre for the DLR, with the present Poplar depot being downgraded to a stabling point.

Only two firms entered the bidding: GEC, which sought to build on its prior business with the DLR, and newcomer BN of Belgium (now a subsidiary of the Canadian rolling stock and aerospace conglomerate Bombardier). BN won the order, and the DLR has since gone on to establish a sound working relationship with the Belgian firm.

BN teamed up with Hawker Siddeley Rail Projects of the UK, with the latter supplying electrical subsystems. Hawker Siddeley subsidiary Brush is providing the traction equipment for the new trains, while sister company Westinghouse Brake and Signal is responsible for the automatic train operation (ATO) equipment. The first batch of 'B' stock will have automatic train protection (ATP) equipment from GEC-General Signal.

While the 'B' stock is of similar design to the earlier trains, some modifications have been made in the light of experience. Visually, the most obvious differences between 'P' and 'B' stock are the external sliding plug doors (made by Deans Powered Doors of Beverley, Humberside), and the use of more transverse seating in the 'B' stock so that there is more room for standing passengers. Some changes have been made with a view to making life easier for the train captains: the door consoles have been moved from over the door to a more convenient position at the side of the door, and the 'B' stock has end doors in case staff should need to move from one

unit in a coupled train to another (coupled operation was never envisaged as a regular occurrence on the 'P' stock). The end doors are not for passenger use and will only be used by staff when the train is stationary. Polyester film has been added to windows to prevent potential shattering.

Some modifications have been made under the floor. Like the 'P' stock, both outer bogies are powered on the 'B' stock — but unlike the earlier stock, there are two sets (rather than just one set) of traction equipment. This means that a failure of one set will not disable a train, and also simplifies maintenance. Regenerative brakes, now an option due to the increased

train frequency on the DLR, are being used on 'B' stock.

The 'B' stock trains are being built at the BN plant in Brugge. The first train was finished at the end of 1990, commissioned in Belgium and delivered to the DLR early in 1991 through the port of Dartford. While the 'P' stock was delivered in halves which were mated together at Poplar, the 'B' stock is being delivered by road as

Below:
General layout of P86 (*below*) and B90 (*bottom*) units. More space is devoted to standees in the later design. *DLR/BN*

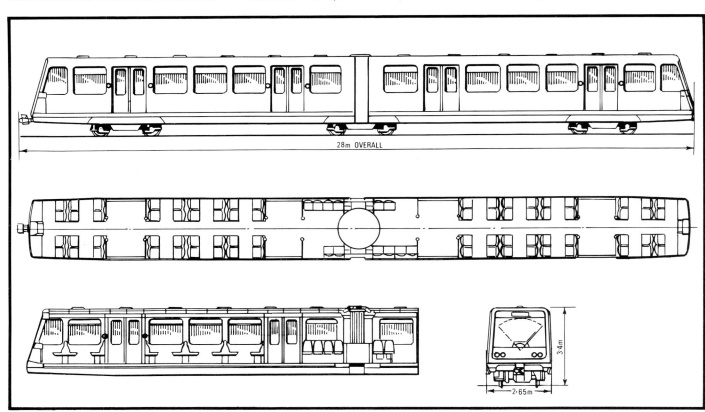

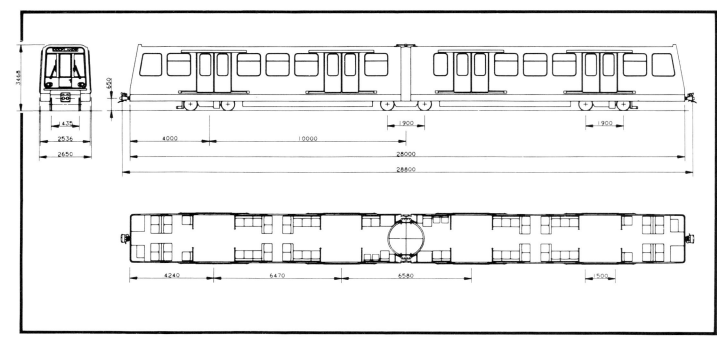

complete trains. Such a large load requires careful routeing over the road system of East London, and close co-operation with the police.

Yet more trains

In 1990, with business on the initial system booming and the Beckton extension looming on the horizon, DLR planners reworked the train operating plan and decided that the 44 trains of 'B' stock on order would be insufficient to run a service on the enlarged system at the frequency desired. Accordingly, in the autumn of 1990 a run-on order of a further 26 vehicles was awarded to BN.

The later vehicles in the 'B' stock order will be equipped to work with the new Alcatel control system being fitted to the Beckton extension, and slated to replace the existing control system on the initial network. Vehicle 25 onwards in the BN fleet will be fitted with Alcatel ATP equipment from the outset (and will be known as B92 stock), while the earlier vehicles (B90s and P89s) will be modified later to work on the new system.

BN now has orders for a total of 70 new vehicles for Docklands which, with the P89 stock, will make a fleet of 80 trains — compared to the 11-train fleet deemed sufficient when the railway was initially

planned. These figures bear ample testimony to the way in which the DLR has completely outgrown the initial concept.

Works vehicles

As the DLR has grown, so has its requirements for works vehicles.

The railway's first maintenance train was a Wickhams CT30 diesel rail crane, which is mated with a flat bed vehicle without through brakes. More recently, the DLR has hired a Ruston 48DS diesel from Grant Lyon Eagre, and this locomotive works with a hopper wagon without through brakes.

At the time of writing, Docklands was acquiring its own second-hand Ruston

---

B90 rolling stock: technical characteristics

General characteristics

Track gauge	1.435m
Body length	28.000m
Body length over coupler	28.800m
Body width over doors	2.650m
Floor height	1.025m
Height rail to roof	3.468m
Wheel diameter new/worn	740/660mm
Doors: number per side	4 double
type	outside sliding
free opening	1,500m
Weight empty	39.3 tonnes
Number of seats	66, plus 4 tip-ups
Standing passengers (6 pass/sq m)	218
Total capacity	284

Performance characteristics

Max service speed	80km/h (50mph)
Acceleration rate	1.1m/sec^2 average
Service deceleration rate	1.3m/sec^2 max
Emergency deceleration rate	1.3m/sec^2
Minimum horizontal radius	38m

Articulation

BN patented wide passage articulation, with full passenger protection and anti-vandalism design

Bogies

2 BN monomotor bogies.
1BN trailer bogie under the articulation.
Elastomeric primary and pneumatic secondary suspension.

Propulsion system and electrodynamic brake

Supplied by BEM (Brush Electrical Machines Ltd)
Power supply: 750V dc third rail.
Motor power continuous rating: 2 x 140kW
Dc chopper controlled propulsion system.
Electrodynamic, regenerative brake

Friction brake equipment

Supplied by WBS (Westinghouse Brake and Signal Ltd).
Discs, air applied for service brake.
Spring applied air released for parking brake.

ATO-equipment

Supplied by WBS (Westinghouse Brake and Signal Ltd). Fully automatic operation controlled by onboard micro-processors containing stored route data.
The whole system is regulated and monitored from a central computer system. The ATP system (supplied by GEC-GS) monitors the speed restriction and intervenes whenever an unsafe condition occurs.

Auxiliary equipment

Solid state 750V dc/28V dc convertor (supplied by Holec).
Heating system: supplied by WBS
Doors and door operators: supplied by WBS

Docklands Light Railway: Stocklist

Class designation	Vehicle Nos	Mechanical equipment	Traction equipment	ATP system	ATO system
P86	1, 2, 3, 4, 5, 6, 7, 8, 9, 10, 11	LHB	GEC	GEC-GS	GEC-GS
P89	12,13,14,15, 16,17,18,19, 20,21	BREL	GEC	GEC-GS	GEC-GS
B90	24 vehicles under construction	BN	HSRP-Brush	GEC-GS	HSRP-Westinghouse
B92	46 vehicles to be constructed	BN	HSRP-Brush	Alcatel	Alcatel

Planned growth of DLR train fleet

DATE	CITY LINE Train length Headway	STRATFORD LINE Train length Headway	VEHICLES REQUIRED (in service/ available)
Nov 90	1 x 6.5min	1 x 6.5min	12/14
Feb 91	1 x 5	1 x 5	15/17
July 91 (1)	2 x 4.5 (3)	1 x 4.5	25/29
Sept 91	2 x 4 (3)	1 x 4	28/33
Apr 92 (2)	2 x 4 (4)	1 x 8 + 2 x 8	31/36
Dec 92 (5)	2 x 2 (6)	1 x 8 + 2 x 8	61/70
Apr 93	2 x 2	2 x 4	68/80

Right:
Chart showing how new trains will be phased into the fleet. The first attempt in August 1990 to introduce more trains into service was beset with problems: hot weather fouled up the points, the ATS played up and there were power supply and earthing difficulties which disrupted the signalling. These problems were addressed and the 6.5min headway service was in place by the end of the year.

Notes:
(1) Opening of first tunnel to Bank
(2) Opening of second tunnel to Bank
(3) Half to Bank, half to Tower Gateway
(4) Threequarters to Bank, quarter to Tower Gateway
(5) Opening of Beckton line
(6) Planning currently involves an 8-min service on the Beckton line until February 1993, being stepped up to a 4-min service then.

88DS, which was due to be delivered in February 1991. This has been refurbished by Alan Keefe of Ross-on-Wye. It has air brake equipment and is able to work with a double flat wagon, being made from two ex-Freightliner flats by BREL Derby. The two 60ft wagons are being shortened and the drawgear ends mated, to give a vehicle with buffers at both ends.

RFS Industries has been contracted to build a four-wheel battery electric locomotive similar to those made for the Channel Tunnel construction work. This vehicle was due to be delivered in June 1991 after manufacture at the Kilnhurst Works of RFS, near Rotherham.

Above right:
Unit 22, the first of the BN-built trains, on a test track in Belgium. *DLR*

Right:
Control unit for manual driving in B90 unit, offset to allow space for end door. *DLR*

Below:
Wickhams CT30 maintenance vehicle, known to DLR staff as 'Sooty'. *David Bateman*

Below right:
B90 unit under construction in the BN works at Brugge, Belgium. *BN*

Bottom:
Inside the shed at Poplar on the day of the Queen's visit to the DLR. *Brian Morrison*

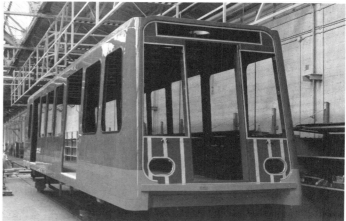

7: DOWN TO BANK

WHEN a handful of North American bankers put their heads together in the early 1980s and recognised the potential for creating a new financial centre in the London Docklands, they were sowing the seeds for a completely changed DLR. The executives at Credit Suisse, First Boston and Morgan Stanley envisaged a new purpose-built office complex which, by comparison with the cramped historic buildings in the City, would have far superior facilities for the computers and other paraphernalia used by today's financial services companies; the only problem was that it would be geographically remote from the centre of the financial industry and would need good transport links.

Thus G. Ware Travelstead, the developer brought in by the banks that set the Canary Wharf ball rolling, had early talks with the nascent DLR management on extending the light railway into the heart of the City at Bank. While Travelstead's interest helped secure a rapid passage of the Bank extension Bill deposited in Parliament in 1985, agreement had still to be reached with the developer on the size of the financial contribution it would be prepared to make. It was not until Olympia & York took over from Travelstead as the developer of the £3 billion Canary Wharf site that a deal was struck.

O&Y agreed to pay roughly half the cost of the Bank extension, contributing £68 million towards the tunnelling work and paying completely for the construction of the new Canary Wharf station in the office complex. To fund its contribution to the DLR, the developer secured a loan from the European Investment Bank — a bank owned by the European Community which grants low-interest loans to promote development in disadvantaged areas.

Construction problems

In July 1987 a contract was signed with Edmund Nuttall Ltd, a British subsidiary of a Dutch construction group, for driving two single-track tunnels from a portal at Royal Mint Street to two new platforms at Bank Underground station (a distance of about three-quarters of a mile). GEC-Mowlem was made responsible for fitting out the tunnels with electrical supplies and so on as part of the Phase II upgrading works.

The 4.9m-diameter running tunnels (about one metre larger than normal tube tunnels) were driven to Bank using a mechanised shield which was also capable of excavating the 7.0m-diameter station tunnels. The lowest part of the new tunnel is 42m below street level and is one of the deepest sections of London's underground railway system; there is a gradient of 6% to take it up to the level of the original DLR.

Beyond the station at Bank, the two tunnels merge into a single overrun tunnel by means of a step-plate junction; this part was driven by a hand shield. The overrun, which ends in a ventilation shaft at Lothbury, allows incoming (westbound) trains to cross over to the outgoing (eastbound) track. Problems were encountered when it was noticed that the

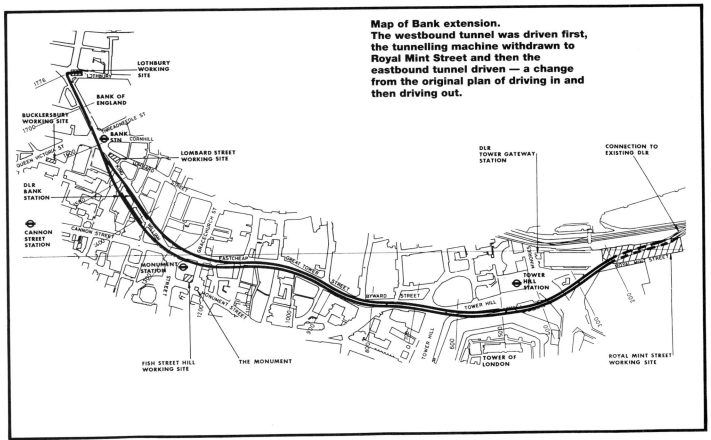

Map of Bank extension.
The westbound tunnel was driven first, the tunnelling machine withdrawn to Royal Mint Street and then the eastbound tunnel driven — a change from the original plan of driving in and then driving out.

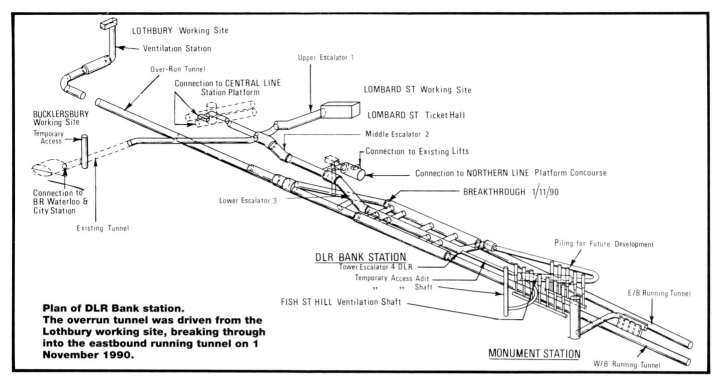

Plan of DLR Bank station.
The overrun tunnel was driven from the
Lothbury working site, breaking through
into the eastbound running tunnel on 1
November 1990.

Labels in diagram: LOTHBURY Working Site — Ventilation Station — Over-Run Tunnel — Connection to CENTRAL LINE Station Platform — Upper Escalator 1 — LOMBARD ST Working Site — LOMBARD ST Ticket Hall — Middle Escalator 2 — Connection to Existing Lifts — Connection to NORTHERN LINE Platform Concourse — BREAKTHROUGH 1/11/90 — BUCKLERSBURY Working Site — Temporary Access — Connection to BR Waterloo & City Station — Lower Escalator 3 — Existing Tunnel — DLR BANK STATION — Tower Escalator 4 DLR — Temporary Access Adit — Shaft — FISH ST HILL Ventilation Shaft — Piling for Future Development — E/B Running Tunnel — MONUMENT STATION — W/B Running Tunnel

overrun tunnel might affect the foundations of the historic Mansion House. Work was delayed while precautionary strengthening measures were undertaken; the breakthrough from the overrun tunnel to the eastbound platform at Bank station was finally achieved on 1 November 1990. This left only the widening out of the step-plate junction and construction of the Central

Line and Waterloo & City Line passage connections for the tunnelling work to be completed.

Track, power and signalling systems were installed in the westbound tunnel by the autumn of 1990, and this was earmarked for opening to the public in July 1991. The other tunnel would be ready by the spring of 1992. Altogether, the Bank

extension fell about 18 months behind time as a result of the Mansion House problem and the inclusion of extra safety features in the wake of the King's Cross Underground fire. It was planned to operate an 8min service to Bank once the first tunnel was opened. This would be stepped up on opening the second tunnel in April 1992, with the ultimate goal a 2min frequency in the peak.

The Olympia & York factor

The DLR has done the most fantastic property enhancement job in creating the conditions for turning a derelict area into a global financial hub, and in tempting one of the biggest property companies in North America (Olympia & York) to throw its weight behind one of the largest (and riskiest) office development projects currently under construction anywhere in the world.

'It is fair to say Canary Wharf happened because of the DLR', says Peter Dale a director at Olympia & York (O&Y) with special responsibility for transport. The automated railway showed a commitment on the part of government bodies to invest not only in public transport, but also in roads, sewers and other infrastructure in the Docklands area.

The speed with which the light railway was built was all-important to the developers. 'In the high risk business of property development, two years is a long time and a decade might as well be forever', according to Michael Schabas, O&Y's vice-president — transport planning. The long timescales common in conventional rail projects could have left Canary Wharf dead in the water.

To keep the momentum going, O&Y has put money into the expansion of the Docklands rail links — around £100 million

after inflation for the DLR, and some £400 million for the Jubilee Line extension. These sums are not to be sniffed at, but they do not make the railways private sector investment projects: about £750 million is being spent on the upgrading and expansion of the DLR (a figure which does not count the Lewisham extension), and O&Y's contribution will amount to only about 15% of the Jubilee Line costs.

By lifting the Docklands rail projects to the top of the queue for government money by putting in a bit of their own, O&Y increased the chances of its £3 billion office block at Canary Wharf being a success. O&Y also gets a say in railway policy: 'Because we have participated in the financing of the railway, we are afforded great courtesy by DLR and LRT management', says Dale. O&Y seconded an employee to the railway for some weeks in 1990 to participate in a reliability study.

While O&Y understands the history of the DLR project ('It was a phenomenally successful implementation — both in time and cost', says Dale), it has not been forgiving of the problems that have beset the railway in the upgrading, and there was some public wrangling in the autumn of 1990 between the DLR and O&Y over the unreliability of the system. Peter Dale later said he was confident that reliability would improve.

Canary Wharf station

The station at the Canary Wharf complex was designed with six platform faces and three tracks, with the idea that when a train enters the station the platform on one side should be used for passengers alighting and the platform on the other for those joining the train. The centre track is intended for trains from the City turning round at Canary Wharf, but has outlets to the south for operational convenience.

The station was partially opened for use by building contractors' staff in April 1991, but opening to the public was put off until the summer, when the first occupiers of the office complex — O&Y itself — were scheduled to move in, to be followed by around 1,200 Morgan Stanley employees in the autumn.

The plan was to close West India Quay station, 100m or so to the north of Canary Wharf station, once the latter was open. With West India Quay closed, work would proceed with quadrupling the short stretch of track from Canary Wharf to the delta junction between the Bank and Stratford lines: the extra tracks would give extra flexibility for coping with a 2min headway service. A private bill had to be put through Parliament to obtain consent for this work, and Royal Assent was expected some time in 1991. The £10 million project should be complete by the end of 1992, with West India Quay being reopened in early 1993.

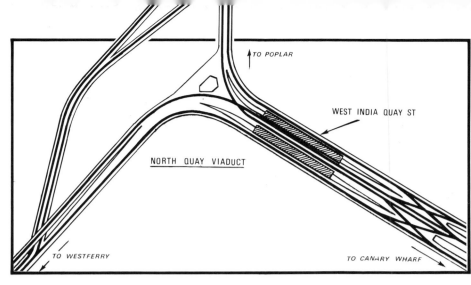

Right:
Track plan of section to be quadrupled through West India Quay.
An alternative plan which would make for a simpler layout here and avoid the need for scissors crossings would involve building a third platform at the next station south from Canary Wharf, Heron Quays — something that might be necessary anyway, due to the growth of patronage in that area.

Below:
Present (*below*) and proposed (*bottom*) new layouts at Leman Street, with and without a new station.
The new design without a station would enable westbound trains for Tower Gateway to be held in the pocket track in the centre while awaiting the road into the terminus, without any need to hold up a following Bank train. If Leman Street station is built, the preferred option is to locate it on the Bank lines only, with no access to Tower Gateway trains.

The shape of the final layout here depends on the future of Tower Gateway; studies suggest that the original terminus must be kept at least until the Jubilee extension is open, as a station at Leman Street would be unable to cope on its own with rush-hour crowds from Canary Wharf in the event of closure of Bank due to a bomb scare or similar occurrence. *DLR*

Changes at Leman Street

The question of what to do with the original terminus at Tower Gateway is a thorny one. Surveys showed that there would be a considerable demand for services from the original terminus once the Bank extension was open, both from tourists who had visited the Tower and then wanted to see Docklands and from business people from that corner of the City. Thus it was planned to retain Tower Gateway once Bank was open, but a project was put in hand to improve the awkward junction at Leman Street. A clause in the Parliamentary bill for the Lewisham extension will make provision for the building of a pocket track here so that Tower Gateway trains could be held to allow a through passage for Bank trains.

The trackwork alterations are not expected to be finished until sometime after the summer of 1992.

One problem with retaining Tower Gateway is that it will not be easy to give it a frequent service, as most trains will be routed to the principal destination at Bank: perhaps only four an hour would be directed to the original terminus. One possible solution would be to build a replacement station at Leman Street, on the Bank tracks. A level stretch of track has been left on the ramp down into the tunnel to Bank for this purpose, but the DLR would have to attract some private money to make building the £3 million station feasible. Developers of vacant sites nearby could be interested in contributing to this project.

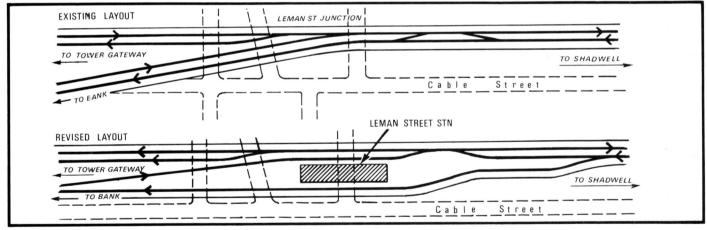

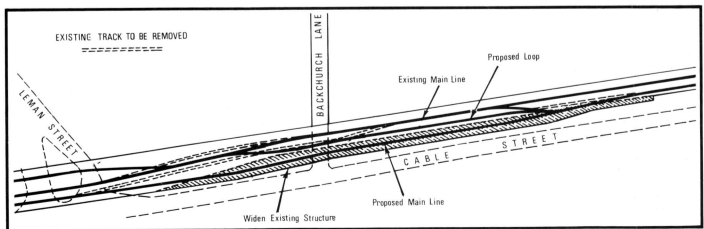

FITTING

Above left:
Leman Street Junction, 16 February 1990. *Brian Morrison*

Left:
Works trains on the 6% grade down into the tunnel to Bank, November 1990. *Brian Morrison*

Above:
Platform tunnel. This has been finished to match Canary Wharf station, with vitreous enamel panels with stainless steel lettering and Swedish granite skirting polished in Italy. There will be a staff presence in the DLR platform area at all times — as there will be at Canary Wharf. *Nuttall*

Below left:
Construction workers in the westbound tunnel. On the right is the conductor rail which, in the tunnel, is not shrouded as there is no need to protect it from the elements. Above this is a dry fire main, which can be filled with water by the London Fire Brigade in 8min in the event of an emergency. Behind the fire main are cable hooks, the bottom one of which is for an earth cable connected to current collection mats under the track. Two-thirds of the way up are brackets for the cables to make the train captains' radios operative in the tunnel. *Brian Morrison*

Below right:
As a back-up to the radios, train captains can use telephones mounted at intervals on the tunnel wall. Lights will be left on at all times, for the psychological benefit of passengers at the front of trains. The evacuation walkway extends the length of the tunnel and can accommodate a wheelchair, upholding the DLR's principle of being usable by the disabled everywhere. Note flag in tunnel ceiling: contractors used a red and yellow flag system for safety protection from works trains in the tunnels. *Brian Morrison*

8: EASTWARDS TO BECKTON

THE Royal Docks area, stretching downriver from the Isle of Dogs, has long been a target of those seeking to renew the urban fabric. The London Transport team looking into light rail for the Docklands in 1980 proposed a route from Aldgate East to Beckton, but when the DLR route map was finally settled it was decided to give precedence to the Isle of Dogs.

As a consequence, while a new city is now rising phoenix-like from the ashes of the West India Docks, that other former hub of Empire — the Royal Docks — remains an urban wasteland, with deserted warehouses standing cheek-by-jowl with disused factories and vacant wharves. This is the area to which the London Docklands Development Corporation is now devoting much of its attention.

A Parliamentary bill for an extension of the DLR to Beckton was first lodged in November 1986, before the initial system was open. The 4.5-mile line would leave the initial system near Poplar, skirt the north side of the old dock basin, and curve round to the north to terminate at Beckton. There was some skirmishing over the route between the LDDC, which favoured a direct east-west line, and local interests championed by Newham Labour MP Tony Banks, who sought to divert the line slightly to serve the existing centre of population at Canning Town. The MP won, and a hump in the line will take it up to serve a station on the big Canning Town roundabout. However, the original aim of a new interchange station serving the North London Link BR line as well as the DLR has

Right:
Aerial view of Royal Docks, August 1990. At right, the King George V and Royal Albert Docks, with City airport in between. The DLR line skirts the western end of the dock (foundation work can be seen in progress) and climbs the partially-completed viaduct to enter the central reservation of the new Royal Albert Dock spine road. In the far top left corner is the site of the future Beckton depot, close to the disused gasworks that posed as a desolate Vietnamese cityscape in the Stanley Kubrick film *Full Metal Jacket*.
DLR

Above:
A special train at Tower Gateway on 19 February 1990, waiting to transport the then Secretary of State for Transport Cecil Parkinson to Naval Row for a start-of-work ceremony for the Beckton extension. *Brian Morrison*

been thwarted as BR was unable to contribute any funds, and a walk under the noisy flyover will be necessary for transfer passengers; in passing, it must be said that it seems unlikely that an opportunity such as this would have been missed in the days of the GLC.

Construction of the extension began in June 1989, with a view to opening in late 1992. Civil engineering contractor for the new line is Taylor Woodrow in a joint venture with initial system veteran Mowlem.

The Beckton extension will cost about £250 million — the much higher per-mile construction cost than the £77 million of the initial system is accounted for only partly by

inflation. Creation of the line in the Royal Docks is more expensive as much new construction is required and there is not the same opportunity to use old railways as there was on the initial system. The extension is also being built to a higher standard, able to cope with two-vehicle trains from Day One and, following complaints about noise on the initial system, with more expensive materials which inhibit noise creation. For instance, concrete beams are being used in preference to steel beams on the elevated sections, and on the Beckton route ballasted track will be used throughout — requiring stronger, more expensive

structures compared to the viaducts on which concrete slab track was used on the initial system.

The Government has decided that no Treasury money will be put into the extension and the £250 million cost is being funded largely by the LDDC, with the outlay to be recouped by sale of Corporation land enhanced in value by the new rail link. The LDDC had to jump through a series of justification hoops to get the go-ahead. 'It was necessary to demonstrate to the satisfaction of the Government that the net cost of the Beckton extension and its subsequent (profitable) operation was justified on economic grounds, allowing for the increase in values of both private and publicly owned land', according to B. T. Collins of the LDDC.

Collins continued: 'It was also necessary for it to pass a far more stringent test — a test which new road schemes do not have to pass. It had to be demonstrated that the increase in value of the land in Corporation ownership was sufficient to fund the 95% of the capital cost of the Beckton extension

Status of Commercial/Industrial Development by area as at 31.03.90

Gross Floor Area by million sq.ft

(Bar chart showing values from 0 to 40 for areas: Royal Docks, Surrey Docks, Isle of Dogs, Wapping/Limehouse)

Status of Development

☒ Completed ☐ Under Construction ☑ Committed ◩ Potential

Left:
The DLR effect:
LDDC planners hope the Beckton extension will stimulate development in the Royal Docks in the way the original DLR has in the Isle of Dogs. *LDDC*

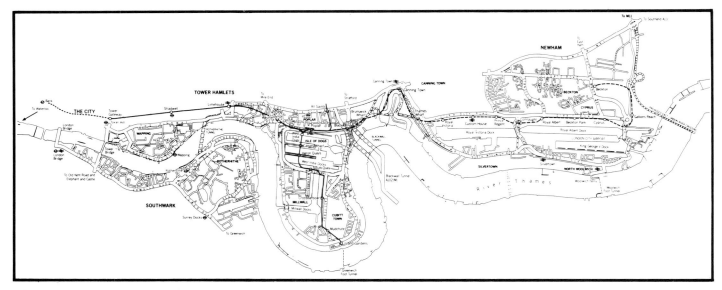

Above:
Map of the Beckton extension. *LDDC*

Right:
DLR Beckton extension trackbed in the central reservation of the new Royal Albert Dock spine road. This January 1991 view was taken from above Cyprus station, looking towards Beckton Park. *Brian Morrison*

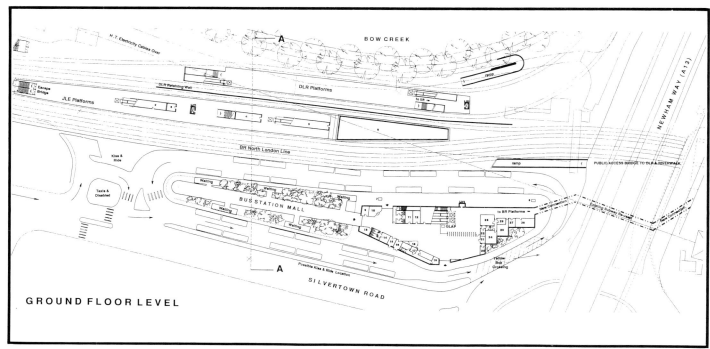

GROUND FLOOR LEVEL

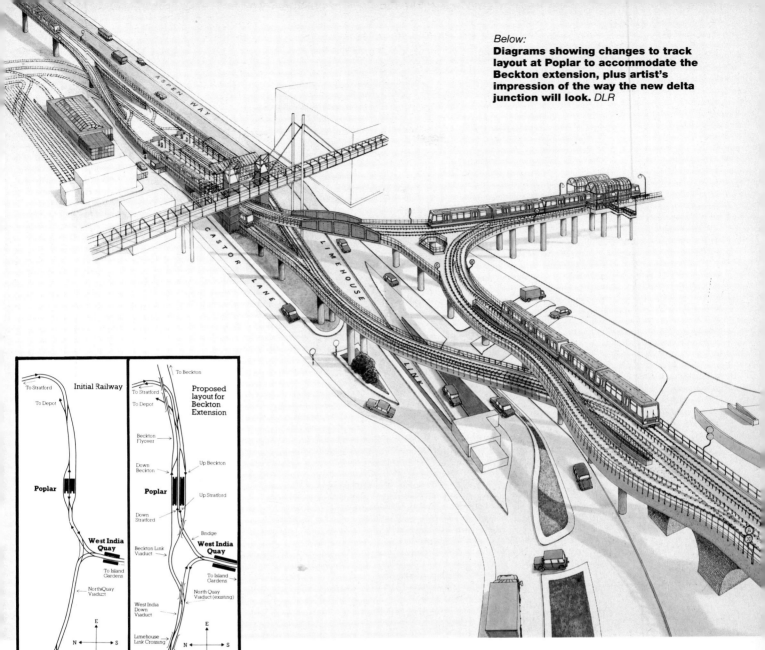

Initial Railway

To Stratford
To Depot

Poplar

West India Quay

To Island Gardens

North Quay Viaduct

E
N — S
W

To City

Proposed layout for Beckton Extension

To Beckton
To Stratford
To Depot

Beckton Flyover

Down Beckton

Up Beckton

Poplar

Up Stratford

Down Stratford

Bridge

Beckton Link Viaduct

West India Quay

To Island Gardens

North Quay Viaduct (existing)

West India Down Viaduct

Limehouse Link Crossing

E
N — S
W

To City

that the Corporation is funding. No new road schemes will ever be built if this onerous test were to be applied in future! It was only because the Corporation's land ownership is very extensive and anticipated land values are high throughout the area that the Beckton extension is now being built.'

As events have turned out, the slump in property values has hit the scheme and the Government has had to provide some extra funding to ensure the branch is completed.

The route

Eleven new stations will have been built along the route of the DLR Beckton extension when it opens. Provision has also been made for two further stations: Thames Wharf, which will be built as part of a development on the Thames Wharf/Limmo site, and Connaught, near the new Connaught road crossing, which will also be built as part of a development on that site.

From Poplar, the railway will run eastwards across Prestons Road, at a height of 9m. It will continue at a height of 12m across the River Lea and drop down to Canning Town. From there it will pass under Silvertown Way and into the Royal Docks.

It will continue across the north side of the Royal Victoria Dock at ground level, rising up to 13m to pass over the Connaught crossing and drop down into a cutting to run between the two carriageways of the new Royal Albert Dock spine road, between Royal Albert and Cyprus stations.

From Cyprus the railway loops around, to the south of the new roundabout at the Gallions pumping station at a height of 9m, and proceeds north, cutting under the Eastern Gateway access road to arrive at the Beckton terminus at ground level.

The new line will not serve directly the London City Airport; traffic at this 'stolport' (short take-off and landing) has not boomed in quite the way that was hoped by its promoters. Silvertown BR station is close to the terminal building; Docklands trains could yet serve the airport if a proposal that the DLR should take over the Canning Town-North Woolwich stretch of the North London Link (which includes Silvertown) comes to pass.

Poplar rollercoaster

Under a separate contract, major works are being undertaken at Poplar to accommodate the Beckton extension. Balfour Beatty is completely rebuilding the station and the junction there — and when the work is complete, DLR trains will fly over and under each other in a spaghetti of steeply-graded lines not wholly unlike a rollercoaster at a funfair.

Onwards to the east?

Beckton will not necessarily be the final eastern terminus of the DLR. The Government has funded various reports into the development of housing on derelict land to the east of the Royal Docks, and the DLR could possibly provide a public transport link here. If the same method of funding were to be used for this extension as was used for the line from Poplar to Beckton, finance could be problematic: 'As the areas are heavily polluted, the basic cost of their development would be high and it would probably be touch and go whether the cost of the further extension of the DLR could be funded fully out of enhanced land values', according to Collins of the LDDC.

One proposal has been that the light railway should be extended as far as Barking, for interchange with London Underground's District and BR's London, Tilbury & Southend (LT&S) lines. If this branch was operated as a self-contained Beckton-Barking shuttle it might reuse the P86 trains.

An extension taking the DLR much further east, to serve the new housing estates at Chafford Hundred, near Grays, was contemplated by consultants considering proposals for upgrading the LT&S line. This idea was rejected as it was felt that Chafford Hundred is too far away from Docklands for what is essentially a local transit system to be adapted to this purpose.

Another idea, put forward by the London Regional Passengers' Committee, would be to put a rail track on the East London River Crossing — a new high level road bridge — so that a new DLR line diverging from the Beckton extension somewhere near Cyprus station could cross over to the south side of the Thames. It seems unlikely this idea will be realised.

This complex new junction has become necessary due to the way in which business has taken off on the DLR. Poplar was originally designed with an 8min service interval in mind for the Stratford and Beckton lines. Canary Wharf has changed all that. Now what is sought is a 4min interval between Stratford and Island Gardens, with a similar service from the Isle of Dogs to Bank — and thus a train every 2min at Canary Wharf.

The LDDC is in favour of a 4min interval on the Beckton line also, and it soon became apparent that with this level of service the original layout at Poplar would require more than minor modification. As a consequence, the junction is being remodelled as shown in the accompanying graphic.

Signalling guinea pig

The Beckton extension will be equipped solely with the new Alcatel control system which is being adopted for the whole network. On the initial system, the Alcatel system is being installed on top of the original GEC-General Signal system, with a changeover likely some time in 1992. As soon as construction is finished, the Beckton line will be put to work as a testbed for the new control system for a few weeks before opening to the public.

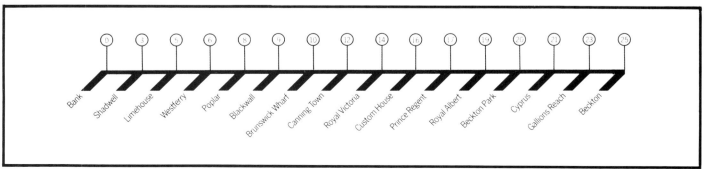

9: UNDER THE RIVER TO LEWISHAM

THE growth of the Docklands Light Railway continues apace: after the extension to Beckton opens in 1992 will come a new 2.5-mile line to Lewisham, south of the River Thames. A Parliamentary bill was deposited in November 1990, and if all goes well the extension will be opened in 1995.

The plan is that the new double-track railway will leave the Isle of Dogs branch of the initial system just north of Mudchute. A new Mudchute station will be built on the new line, plus a new Island Gardens station underground; this will allow the stretch of single-track railway down to the present terminus to be closed. The extension will continue in tunnel under the Thames. Another underground station — named 'Cutty Sark' — will be built in Greenwich town centre, saving the name 'Greenwich' for an interchange with the BR station of that name at the point where the underground line comes to the surface. From there the extension will follow a small river, the Ravensbourne, with stations at Deptford Bridge and Elverson Road, terminating at Lewisham BR station.

Widespread benefits

Two-vehicle trains at 4min headways, with a capacity to carry 6,000pph, are envisaged for the Lewisham extension in the peak, with a 10min interval service in the off-peak. Substantial numbers of people will benefit from the new link. Commuters from Kent and southeast London who currently have to make a dogleg journey into the centre of London and out again to reach offices in Docklands will have a much easier journey on the new line, changing at Lewisham or Greenwich. This will ease overcrowding on lines into the central London termini, and on the Bank section of the DLR.

With a journey time of 16min from Lewisham to Canary Wharf, the tunnel will boost the number of people within 45min travelling time of the Isle of Dogs from 1.5 million to 2 million. This will improve the economic prospects for office developments in Docklands.

Journeys further afield will also be facilitated: trips to Stansted airport and much of East Anglia will be possible by changing at Stratford, while Limehouse will give access to Tilbury line services. Easier journeys to Kent and the southeast will be possible in the reverse direction.

The councils south of the river, Lewisham and Greenwich, are hopeful that the extension will bring extra business to their areas. Deptford is in particular need, having been identified by the Government as an inner city area that should have priority for renewal. The extension will improve access to attractions south of the river, such as the huge shopping complex at Lewisham and the historical area of Greenwich, which attracts 1.5 million tourists each year.

Private financing

A novel form of financing has been adopted for the Lewisham extension. The intention is that it will be built under a design, build, own, toll and transfer (Dbott) contract — a refinement of the design-and-build contract used for the initial system. A drawback with a simple design-and-build contract is that there is too little obligation on the contractor should things go awry once the building phase is over. Under Dbott, it is intended that the winning bidder for the contract should construct the new railway and be responsible for its operation.

Plainly, it would be preferable for trains from Lewisham to interwork with the rest of the DLR rather than there being an enforced change from the trains of one company to another at Mudchute — so in practice, it is likely that the builder of the Lewisham line

Below:
Aerial view of Lewisham station. Running across the centre of the picture in the background is the line to Bexleyheath and Dartford, while on the left are the lines to Orpington, next to which the DLR platforms will be situated. The bus station close by will make this a comprehensive interchange point. *David Brown*

View looking westwards from the down platform at Greenwich station. The DLR will surface in the area behind the railings on the left of this picture. David Brown

Right:
Map showing route of Lewisham extension.
Since this map was prepared, the preferred name of the Deptford station has been changed to 'Deptford Bridge'.
LT

will subcontract operation to the DLR, charging a toll for each train using its tracks. At the end of a concession period this arrangement would end and ownership of the Lewisham line would be transferred to the DLR.

Another possible, but unlikely, outcome is that the builder of the new line would subcontract operation to a company other than the DLR — in conjunction with that other company taking over the operation of the rest of the DLR. Who might such a company be? Olympia & York, the most obvious contender as a private operator, is

Below:
Diagram showing position of Lewisham DLR platforms in relation to BR station. An exit at the south end will provide convenient access to the town centre.
DLR

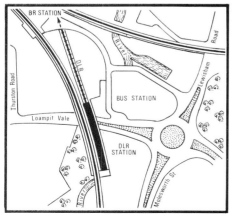

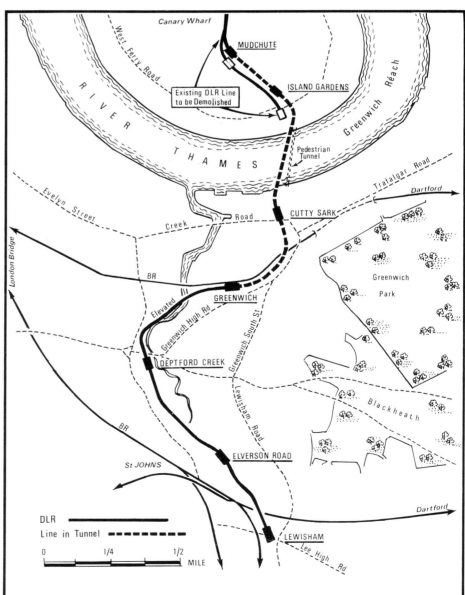

Above:
The single-track approach to Island Gardens station. This section of track will be abandoned, replaced by a double-track underground approach to the Thames tunnel. *Brian Morrison*

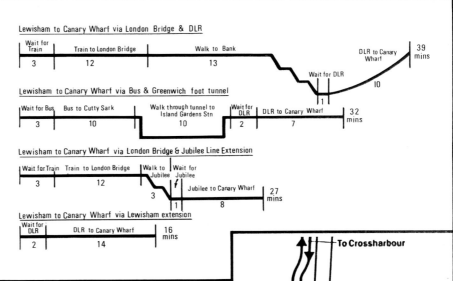

Lewisham to Canary Wharf via London Bridge & DLR

| Wait for Train | Train to London Bridge | Walk to Bank | | DLR to Canary Wharf | 39 mins |
| 3 | 12 | 13 | Wait for DLR / 10 | | |

Lewisham to Canary Wharf via Bus & Greenwich foot tunnel

| Wait for Bus | Bus to Cutty Sark | Walk through tunnel to Island Gardens Stn | Wait for DLR | DLR to Canary Wharf | 32 mins |
| 3 | 10 | 10 | 2 | 7 | |

Lewisham to Canary Wharf via London Bridge & Jubilee Line Extension

| Wait for Train | Train to London Bridge | Walk to Jubilee | Wait for Jubilee | Jubilee to Canary Wharf | 27 mins |
| 3 | 12 | 3 | 1 | 8 | |

Lewisham to Canary Wharf via Lewisham extension

| Wait for DLR | DLR to Canary Wharf | 16 mins |
| 2 | 14 | |

not interested: although it did step in to save the ailing riverbus operation, O&Y does not see itself as a transport operator and would prefer to work with the existing DLR management.

Nor is any other company likely to be interested, despite privatisation of the DLR having been a dream of the Conservative government ever since the light railway was authorised. At present, the financial equations do not add up: one source estimates that recovery of the DLR's costs at the farebox in 1989-90 was about 57% (the shortfall being made up from LT funds).

While operation looks likely to remain in public hands, the Dbott system should see a private company financing the building of the Lewisham extension. It will cost about £130 million; the boroughs of Lewisham and Greenwich have agreed to chip in about £5 million apiece, but the rest has to be found privately. One advantage of the Dbott system is that it means the international money markets can be tapped for investment finance for the DLR; as a state-owned company, LT is not allowed to raise funds in the City, while a private company is not hamstrung in the same way. Considerable international interest was aroused among construction companies and finance houses by the Dbott contract; the DLR planned to issue tender documents during 1991. It was hoped that the competition would elicit some innovative ideas from those tendering.

Just where the acquisition of rolling stock fits into the Dbott process is not yet clear. Between six and 10 extra trains will

be needed for the Lewisham extension, and if they were to be built from new, orders would probably have to be placed towards the end of 1992. It would be no surprise to see a decision to strip out the P86s and refit them with materials which made them suitable for underground working.

Reverse direction flows
The Lewisham extension should provide a big boost for the DLR. 'In transport planning terms it is very effective', says DLR Managing Director John Bygate. 'It will be backfeeding the original part of the DLR, and effectively doubles peak capacity.'

Further benefits could be derived by extending the line on from Lewisham to Bromley, using Network SouthEast's Bromley North branch for part of the route. This idea, suggested in the South London Assessment Study of transport needs in the south of the capital, remains one for consideration in the future.

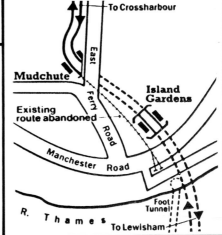

Centre:
Diagram showing way in which DLR will shorten journey times.
London Borough of Lewisham

Above:
Diagram showing changes to track layout planned at Island Gardens. *DLR*

10: THE HUMAN FACE OF THE DLR

THE Docklands Light Railway is an automated railway, but unlike the automatic railway just across the Channel in Lille, each train is staffed. The staff member, known as a train captain, does not (under normal circumstances) drive the train, but operates the doors, answers passengers' queries and checks tickets.

As this is a customer contact job as much as a railway operating post, train captains are as likely to have a background in retailing or restaurant work as to have worked on the Underground or for British Rail. A substantial number of the train captains are women (and when train captains are referred to in the masculine gender below, the reader should take this as a generic for 'he' or 'she'). One requirement in the recruitment process has been that applicants must live in the Docklands, helping staff to identify the DLR as 'their' railway.

In their smart light blue DLR uniforms, the train captains look a breed apart from Underground staff. They are not represented by the same unions: the DLR's staff voted in favour of setting up their own staff association which represents them on non-wage issues, while (at the time of writing) the electricians' union EETPU negotiates about wages.

Just what is it like to work as a train captain? To find out, I accompanied Jim McAlpine, a train captain of some six months' standing and a former merchant seaman, on a day-shift in November 1990. My overwhelming impression from the day is that there is much more human judgement required in the operation of the railway than might be thought necessary for an automatic system — and that the train captain's role is far from just being a happy smiling face welcoming passengers on to the trains!

Trouble at mill

When I joined Capt McAlpine at West India Quay on a train going south to Island Gardens, there were problems — unfortunately, this is a far from uncommon experience, as the light rail system is struggling to accommodate many more passengers than the number for which it was designed. A faulty train had been taken out of service on the southern branch, and

the manoeuvre of shunting it into a siding at Crossharbour had delayed other services. As we sped south towards Island Gardens, big queues of northbound commuters had built up on the opposite platforms as a result of the gap in the service. 'We find we get a lot of abuse when people have been waiting', McAlpine remarked ruefully.

As it turned out, we escaped being on the receiving end of bad language: a unit preceded us northwards, and the unfortunate captain of that train would have had to face the impatient crowds. With the trains all out of sync, 'Our main priority now is catching up', explained McAlpine, to help shift the eastbound throng that would have built up at Tower Gateway, our next destination. Accordingly, McAlpine made

getting swiftly away from stations his first consideration, with ticket inspection temporarily assuming a secondary importance.

On arrival at a station, passengers can operate individual doors with nearby buttons. A green light on the console above the door informs the train captain that the track ahead of the train is clear, and the computer is ready to depart when he is. Train captains operate two separate buttons to close, first, the bulk of the doors

Below:
Train captain at Poplar, January 1991.
Brian Morrison

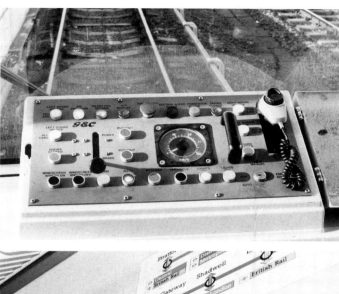

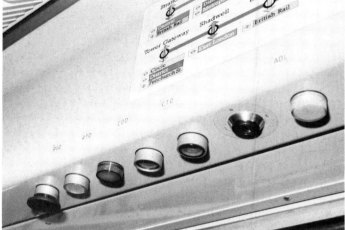

Above:
Control room at Poplar. Controllers are in radio contact with train captains, and can call up pictures of station platforms on TV screens. *Brian Morrison*

in the train, and then the one at which the train captain is standing. The operation is completed by checking for the 'ADL' (All Doors Locked) light, which signifies that the central computer has received the signal that it is now safe to move the train on to the next station.

On the initial 21 trains built by LHB and BREL the doors (designed for lower passenger numbers than those currently experienced) fold inwards, meaning that the train captains are constantly reminding people to be careful that they are not hit by an opening door. The new BN trains will have sliding doors on the outside of the vehicle and will not face this problem; sliding doors similar to those on D78 Underground stock will be retrofitted to the existing trains.

The BREL trains that entered service in 1990 have a new feature much welcomed by the train captains: a bell rings when the RTD (Ready to Depart) light goes green, informing the captain that he should close the doors as soon as feasible. 'It's only a little modification, but it saves the wear on your neck!' commented Capt McAlpine, referring to the need to be constantly looking up at the overdoor console on the original trains for the RTD light.

'You've got to keep to that RTD', remarked McAlpine, explaining that the control room at Poplar is monitoring the movement of trains around the DLR and will contact a train captain on the radio if his train stands at a station for a long while with a green RTD light. However, the control room staff are often unable to appreciate fully what is going on at the sharp end. For instance, a passenger may be hovering half in and half out of the door, uncertain if he is going the right way and asking for directions to an obscure destination: 'Then it is a choice of being rude to the customer or not keeping to time', said McAlpine.

Revenue protection

With the train service settling back into normal, McAlpine was able to devote more attention to revenue protection duties, inspecting tickets between stations. It can be something of a juggling act to combine the two duties, especially when there is a problem with a ticket — as then the train captain has to rush to and fro between passenger and door console.

On the morning I travelled with Jim McAlpine, there were no cases of fraudulent travel — but there was a problem with bogus change from a ticket machine. Petty criminals have established a way of getting 10p pieces to pass as 50p pieces in the ticket machine, meaning honest passengers are shortchanged by 40p when the coins pass out of the ticket machine as change. DLR staff were working on ways of

Top:
Train console for manual driving. Power is controlled by a lever beneath the GEC logo; the 'Section Ahead Clear' light above the speedometer acts as in-cab signalling. *Brian Morrison*

Above:
Overhead console, P86 stock. From left, the controls and lights are: emergency stop plunger (known as 'mushroom'); ROD — reopen doors; RTD — ready to depart light; COD — close other doors; CTD — close this door; keyhole, with I — inhibit, N — normal and E — energise (door controls) positions; ADL — all doors locked. The 'I' key position illuminates a red light to the right of this view: it is used to immobilise the train should the train captain need to leave the vehicle. *Brian Morrison*

preventing this fraud (and indeed a wholesale renewal of ticket machines was on the cards) but, at the time of my visit, train captains — the human faces of the railway — were having to deal with the situation as best they could. As train captains do not carry a cash float and thus are unable to rectify a problem such as this on the spot, some filling in of forms was required to obtain a refund. Completing the forms while managing the doors required some nifty footwork on the part of Jim McAlpine.

Into manual mode

The segregation of the DLR's right of way enabled automatic operation to be adopted on the new light railway, but a console was built into the trains for manual operation should the need arise. The need has arisen more than was probably envisaged at the outset. Manual mode is used whenever there is a possibility of people or objects being on the track — whether the problem be trespassers, maintenance staff or windblown debris — and a pair of human eyes is essential. Manual is adopted as soon as there is a report of somebody or something on the track; train captains may radio in to request manual operation should they spot something themselves. It may be used as a precaution, as for instance during the gales of the 1990 winter, when there was a high likelihood of the track being obstructed.

On my trip with Jim McAlpine, maintenance staff working on the failed train stabled at Crossharbour necessitated a spell in manual mode. Two forms of manual operation are possible: ATP (automatic train protection) manual, where the train can be driven at speeds up to the limit for the line; and shunt, where speeds are limited to 20km/h.

In the shunt mode, which is normally confined to depot use, the computer gives no protection. On 22 April 1991, two DLR trains were in a slow-speed collision at West India Quay when one was being driven in shunt mode due to the signalling being out of action. While the Inspecting Officer's report on the accident had yet to be produced when this book went to press, it was most likely that this accident was a straight case of human error — and did not point to a fault in the safety system of the computer.

To avoid accidents like this, ATP manual is the usual form adopted for driving out on the line. To drive in this way, the train captain needs three lights lit up on the

Below:
These boards in the four-foot at stations are for drivers using the manual controls; they indicate the stopping point to line the train up with the data docking link. *Brian Morrison*

Above:
Talking shop at Tower Gateway. *Brian Morrison*

console: 'ATP manual', 'Section Ahead Clear' (a form of cab signal, equivalent to a single yellow on BR), and 'Doors Closed'. With all three lights, the train captain can apply the power controller to move the train.

Should the 'Section Ahead Clear' light go out en route, the train captain will stop the train at the next trackside route board — a circle with a cross through it — indicating the border between two signalling sections. In the event that he does not so stop the train, the ATP mechanism in the central computer will come into play, automatically stopping the train.

When driving, train captains have to watch carefully for trackside boards marked with a plain 'G' or crossed 'G', the former marking the start of a section where there is a gap in the conductor rail and the train will not be able to restart should it be stopped; the latter board marks the end of the gap. In the event of a train becoming 'gapped', a time-consuming rescue operation has to be performed, usually with the following train pushing the stationary train forward until it regains the conductor rail.

Once the maintenance staff were off the line, automatic operation was resumed, and McAlpine returned to his duties closing doors, checking tickets and being the human face of the railway. But as I discovered on my morning excursion, Jim McAlpine and his colleagues are not just smiling faces — the rigour of operating the Docklands Light Railway requires a lot more than that.

My thanks to Jim McAlpine for allowing me to share his morning.

Above:
A view at Island Gardens showing boards marking the gap in the conductor rail. *A. C. Mott*

11: A MATURING SYSTEM

THE Docklands Light Railway is a railway in transition. The 11-train, 7.5-mile initial system which cost £77 million, is being transformed into a 15.5-mile system which will use more than 80 trains and will have cost almost £1 billion.

Overseeing this transition requires a huge management effort. There are the extensions to Bank, Beckton and Lewisham; the rollercoaster interchange at Poplar; and quadrupling of the track at West India Quay. Underground working is being introduced to the system, and there are plans for a revised junction layout at Leman Street. The train fleet is being quadrupled in size, and regenerative braking introduced for the first time. A new signalling and control system is coming in, based not on traditional track circuits but on the novel moving block system. A new station is planned for Stratford.

Contractors are beavering away at separate parts of this ambitious programme, and the grand design is being drawn together at the DLR's headquarters in Poplar. 'Our main task in engineering is to prevent too many people trying to do too many things to a very tiny railway: you can only make a limited number of changes to the system without causing confusion', says Managing Director John Bygate. On the operating side, the DLR has been busy building up numbers of personnel, especially middle managers, to cope with the increasing frequency of services and to deal with the influx of new trains.

There is, however, an end in sight. The Docklands Light Railway will not be the growing railway for ever: it is after all a local transit system, and maturity looms. While several ideas for extending the railway further have been canvassed, insiders give a likelihood of success to only two: a takeover of British Rail's North London Link to North Woolwich, and a new line from Beckton to Barking (although this latter could take years, or even decades, to realise). London Transport is undertaking a study of the best way of serving the southern part of the Royal Docks and takeover of the North London Link from Canning Town to North Woolwich by either the Jubilee Line or the DLR is among the options being studied.

It seems unlikely now that the DLR will go to three-car operation: space has been left at stations for extending platforms to

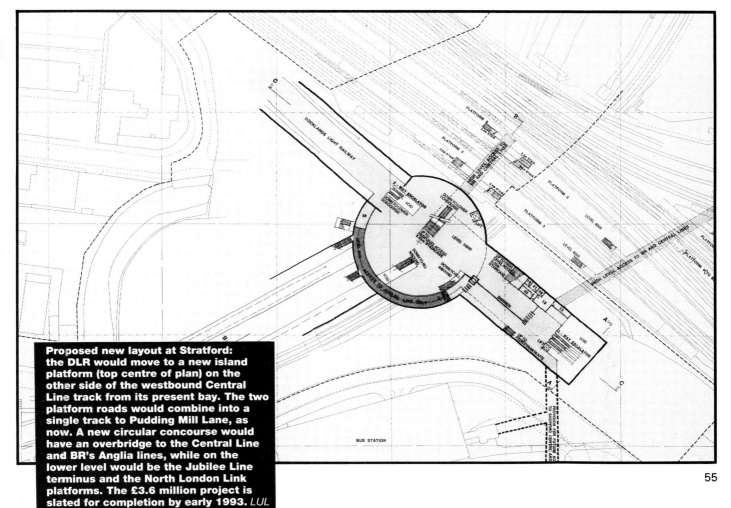

Proposed new layout at Stratford: the DLR would move to a new island platform (top centre of plan) on the other side of the westbound Central Line track from its present bay. The two platform roads would combine into a single track to Pudding Mill Lane, as now. A new circular concourse would have an overbridge to the Central Line and BR's Anglia lines, while on the lower level would be the Jubilee Line terminus and the North London Link platforms. The £3.6 million project is slated for completion by early 1993. *LUL*

three cars if necessary, but the thinking behind this was as a fallback option in case the Jubilee Line was not built. With the Jubilee having the capacity to shift over 20,000pph in each direction from 1996 onwards, the DLR will take on a secondary role. It is a fine irony: extension of the Jubilee to Docklands was always the goal of transport planners, with the light railway originally seen as very much a second best — but the DLR has sparked the economic transformation in the Docks that has now made the first best possible.

A fine transport system

The coming of the Jubilee Line will signal the beginning of a new era for the Docklands rail system, plugging it into the main tube network in central London. There will immediately be first-class links with the West End, Waterloo (for Channel Tunnel trains to the Continent) and London Bridge to add to those already provided by the DLR.

Canary Wharf will be at the centre of this system. Not only will the office complex have its own station on the Jubilee Line and the Isle of Dogs branch of the DLR, but it will be within walking distance of Poplar station — thus making all trains on the DLR accessible to the 50,000 office workers there. Commuters from Essex and Kent, the traditional dormitories for the clerical workers in the financial industry, will be able to reach Canary Wharf via the DLR interchanges at Stratford, Lewisham and Greenwich; peak flows will spread to all four points of the compass and will not be confined to one particular direction.

Construction of CrossRail under the centre of London will allow an easy commute from the Thames Valley and the Chilterns to Docklands by changing to the DLR at Stratford. Who knows: if one private consortium's proposal of a high speed line from the Channel Tunnel to a terminal at Stratford comes to pass, Docklands could become an easy commute this way from northern France!

He may have a vested interest, but Peter Dale of Olympia & York makes no empty boast when he says of Docklands that 'It will be one of the best rail-served locations in London'.

Below:
Poplar yard on opening day, 30 July 1987. *Brian Morrison*

References

Bayman, R. and Jolly, S. *Docklands Light Railway — Official Handbook* (Capital Transport Publishing, 1988)
Collins, B. T. 'Light Transit to Stimulate Development: the London Docklands Experience' in *Light Transit Systems in British Cities* (Thomas Telford, 1990)
Ellmers, C. 'Docklands Past and Present' in *Guide to London Docklands* (Curtis, 1989)
Ford, R. 'The Technology of Docklands', *Modern Railways* May 1985; 'The Way Ahead — Docklands Light Railway', *Modern Railways* August 1987; 'Informed Sources', *Modern Railways* September 1987
Heaps, C. 'Docklands — The Growing Railway', *Modern Railways* April 1990
Houlder, V. 'Canary Wharf's Future is Still Up in the Air'. *The Financial Times* 8 November 1990.
Schabas, M. 'Light Rail Transit to Stimulate Development: The Developer's Perspective' in *Light Transit Systems in British Cities* (Thomas Telford, 1990)
Twelftree, P. D. 'The role of Rail Access in the Regeneration of London's Docklands' in *Transit 2020: Planning, Financing, Design and Operation of Railways Worldwide* (IMechE, 1990)
Wyse, W. J. 'DLR Update', *Modern Tramway* January 1991.
Smart Transit Systems: Present Status — Future Prospects; London Docklands Light Railway. Working Paper No 19'. (Ecoplan International, 1990).